# The Rule
# of
# Saint
# Benedict

Abbot Parry OSB
&
Esther de Waal

First published in 1990
Reprinted 1990, 1993, 1995, 1997 & 2000


Gracewing
2 Southern Avenue, Leominster
Herefordshire HR6 0QF

ISBN 0 85244 168 1


Additional typesetting by Action Typesetting Ltd,
Gloucester, GL1 1SP


Printed by Redwood Books
Trowbridge, Wiltshire, BA14 8RN

I am writing these instructions to you, so that . . . you may know how to behave in the household of God.

I Tim 3:14–15 (RSV)

. . . so that no one may be upset or saddened in the household of God.

The Rule of St Benedict (Ch.31)

# Preface

'Who is the man who desires to see Good Days?' Normally when a young man or a young woman decides to enter a monastery, friends and relatives do not immediately conclude that he or she is seeking a good time. They are more likely to think that their friend takes a poor view of life's possibilities. Yet in the Prologue to the Rule we find St Benedict quoting the Scripture: 'Who is the man who desires life and is eager to see Good Days?' (Ps 33:12). Evidently he believes that he has something of real value to offer, and he continues: 'What can be sweeter to us than the voice of the Lord as he invites us, dearest brothers? See how in his loving mercy the Lord points out to us the Way of Life.' The expression recalls how Christ called himself the Way (Jn 14:6) and the earliest Christians referred to themselves simply as followers of the Way (Acts 9:2). Before we examine St Benedict's exposition of how to follow the Way, a few words on the man himself may be useful.

The traditional dates for the life of St Benedict are 480–547. The only early account of his life that we have is that given by St Gregory, Pope, 590–604. St Gregory drew information from persons who had known St Benedict personally. But the concept of how to write a biography differed so much in the sixth century from what we expect in the twentieth that St Gregory's account is today accepted only with considerable reserve. Moreover a careful examination of what he does tell us is leading some modern scholars[1] to place St Benedict's life rather

---

[1] *La Règle de Saint Benoît* (1980) tr. and ed. H. Rochais and E. Manning. Paris, Edition du Centenaire, Desclée de Brouwer, 1980.

later, say about 520–575. The salient outline is not in dispute.

Born of an honourable family of Nursia in Tuscany, he studied in his youth at Rome. Disgusted by the decadent culture that he found there, he departed, still very young, seeking God in solitude in the mountains round Subiaco, fifty miles to the west of Rome. While he was still quite young, a local monastery invited him to be its abbot. He accepted, but the experiment did not last long, and he willingly returned to his solitude. There disciples came to him and he became the founder of a monastery, and lived, it seems, in the ruins of Nero's villa, bordering on a lake (Sub-lacu). A second time he encountered opposition, this time apparently from outside the monastery. So he migrated southward and established himself on Monte Cassion, overlooking the road between Rome and Naples. Here, making extensive use of materials already in existence, he composed the Rule on which his fame rests.

If we want to know his personality it is really to this document we must turn. Its Prologue shows that the youthful urge to brook no delay, which had led him to abandon his Roman studies, still lived on in the mature man. For him, 'the way of God's Commandments' is 'run in a sweetness of love that is beyond words', and the Gospel command 'Walk while you have the light' (Jn 12:35) appears in the Prologue changed, no doubt unconsciously, into 'Run while you have the light.'

We may note here that a modern reader perusing the Rule for the first time might conclude from the mass of Scripture texts fired at him, that St Benedict lacked originality. It is well then to underline that if this man is always quoting Scripture it is because its teachings and its very words have become the texture of his mind. His invariable approach to every problem is to ask: 'What does the Lord say about this?' And for him that is the key to the answer. Hence he expresses his doctrine quite naturally by weaving together those scriptural texts which have formed his mind.

Although we think of St Benedict as a founder, if only because the majority of those who follow his Rule are called Benedictines, in reality his position in history is not as simple as that. The monastic life had already had a history of two hundred years, and in his day it was already widespread in both the Eastern and Western parts of the Church. Benedict then entered the ranks of an existing institution and produced a rule based on his knowledge of what was happening around him as well as on his own experience at Subiaco and Monte Cassino. The text which he left behind him was seen as a *Summa* of the best monastic wisdom of his day, and it would remain a central document by which future generations of monks would guide themselves.

The reader who does not belong to the monastic order, but reads the Rule as one among other spiritual classics, may find it by comparison with other inspired spiritual writings rather a matter-of-fact document. It is indeed a restrained and balanced one, but to understand it the reader must accept its point of view. It is not just spiritual teaching, nor just a personal code, but it aims to set up a whole society (if a small one) that is truly Christ-centred, and provided with the legislation that will, as far as any legislation can, keep it on course. This requires both depth of spiritual teaching and a balanced recognition of the needs of human nature. If it has survived for so many centuries, its survival is due to the combination of the two elements: experience of the actualities of human life in community and the insights of one to whom 'nothing is to be preferred to Christ'. St Benedict brought both characteristics to bear in constructing his 'household of God'.

The Rule is not intended to displace in any way the Gospel from the centre of the way of life of this monastic society. On the contrary the Gospel is the supreme rule. 'It is under its guidance that we pursue our way' (Prol.), and the function of the Rule is to enable us to apply the fullness of the Gospel teaching to the actual circumstances of daily life, not only on the level of the response of the individual, but also through the attitude of society. For this purpose it draws heavily on previous experience and on the writings of the Fathers of the Church.

Experience teaches negative as well as positive lessons. And the first Chapter of the Rule takes a look round the monastic world as St Benedict saw it in his day. He found a good deal in which the results did not correspond to the ideal. So the Rule discarded much that was seen to have no permanent value, and set out to build a monastery that would be both solid and fruitful in its spiritual formation. The quest for stability is basic to its thinking: yet it presented a balance of flexibility largely because it left a wide sphere open to the judgement of the Abbot, and so could remain a usable guide through all succeeding centuries until this one. Indeed, in different ages and places one may observe major departures from what the Rule laid down; yet sooner or later there is a return to a closer interpretation. It is perhaps through this rhythm in which adaptation and a return to the closer observance follow each other, that each succeeding generation of monks keeps the Rule alive in history. It is not a matter of alternations of strictness and laxity in observance, but of adaptation, greater or less, to the climate of the spiritual world of each age or to the local needs of the Church.

In constructing the society, Benedict follows a three-fold line of thought.

Firstly, he is a teacher of monastic doctrine. As we have already said, this doctrine did not supplant the Gospel. At this level the Rule embodies certain maxims laid down as a fruit of experience, and certain virtues without which the pursuit of the Gospel would be an illusion and the desire for union with God a path of self-deception. There was nothing new in the teachings; it was the fruit of experience: thus the longest Chapter of the Rule (VII) is about Humility and the theme runs through all the others. Another equally radical chapter is on Obedience (V), for the practice of obedience was seen as inseparable from that of humility. A third chapter dealt with the practice of Silence (VI). This may seem a more technical matter, but it was seen as a safeguard to the practice of other necessary things (recollection in prayer) both for the individual and the society as a whole. A lengthy chapter on 'The Tools of Good Works' (IV) may seem to contain much that is obvious from both the Old and New Testaments, but there are many moments in a man's life when such reminders are more useful than more elevated sentiments.

The reader should note, however, that while spiritual teaching predominates in the earlier chapters, it is not confined to them. Spiritual teaching occurs throughout the Rule even in the most prosaic matters (e.g. Ch. LVII 'The Craftsmen of the Monastery' and Ch. XL 'The Measure of Drink'). The concluding chapters of the Rule are particularly significant in this respect. While the spiritual teaching of the Rule is both rich and balanced, teaching alone does not set up a society.

The second element the Rule provides for is the structure of the House of God: the Abbot as the father; the monks with their equality as brethen (Ch. II); the community to be consulted in grave matters (Ch. III); the senior monks to be consulted in lesser ones. A wide sphere of temporal cares is assigned to the cellarer, with significant instructions (Ch. XXXI); other officials are established, also with appropriate instructions (e.g. Ch. LXVI, 'The Doorkeepers'). There is discussion on the desirability of appointing a Prior (Ch. LXV, the Rule betrays uncertainty here) and the order of the Brethren in community. These and other matters are legislated for, and are clearly of great significance in the construction of the way of life of the monastery. They are still formative in monastic society.

The third strand in the organisation established by the Rule is that of observances. These begin with Ch. VIII, in which chapter and the following ones Benedict lays down in great detail how and when the Divine Office is to be said. This is followed by several chapters of the Penal Code and then more detailed regulations for the monastic day and for various places of the monastery, for the treatment of newcomers, guests etc. Indeed, the central stretch of the Rule ranged through all the practical aspects of how the life is to be carried out. Regulations, however, are often explained by doctrinal teachings, and even when this is not done, such doctrinal reasons are not far to seek. Thus there is to be strict silence after Compline (Ch. XLII); this was undoubtedly thought of, not merely as a rule, but a co-operation with the divine plan, which assigned activity to the day, and intended the night for repose, and therefore for complete silence. The fact that the Rule is read aloud in monasteries (Ch. LXVI) means that even when variations are made, the mind of the legislator can never be forgotten.

The amount of space St Benedict devotes to organising the Divine Office is significant of the importance he attached to it. Nor was it merely a matter of long vocal prayer. For the early monks understood prayer to be the principal means for attaining union with God, and union with God was the end of human living and therefore of the monastic organisation. It should be noted that while Chs. VIII–XX are all about prayer, the subject recurs again and again in the Rule. It is hardly too much to say that it gives meaning to the whole.

The little chapter on when Alleluia is to be said (XV), should not be passed over as insignificant; on the contrary, it reminds us how important the theme of the Resurrection was in the lives of the monks, and how they illustrated this.

For the life of the monk was not just a programme of aspirations for moral improvement. Spiritual progress meant a closer 'incorporation in Christ', and this in turn implied living with the thought of the Paschal Mystery in mind. That Mystery reached its consummation in the Resurrection. So this chapter enacted that the Resurrection should be recalled, as day succeeded day.

The section that is likely to cause most raising of eyebrows to the modern reader is that of the Penal Code (Chs. XXII–XXX). And there is more of it later (Chs. XLIII–XLVI). To understand this at all we have to grasp the point of view of the sixth-century legislator who is organising a young, vigorous society and conscious of the need to protect it against falling away and corruption. To do this he makes use of such means as were current in his day. Nobody would have questioned it then; equally, nobody would want it unadapted now. Yet it should be noted that a society with definite standards of life which it cherishes, does in all ages have to take appropriate action to defend them. We as a society seem to be reaching a period of real weakness today, as we become more uncertain about the structure and standards of our society. The point of view of the Rule is that the standards of community life have to be guarded with great care.

The Rule then combines these three lines of thought. Some chapters are clearly devoted to one rather than to another, but often they are mingled. Always the intention is to provide a framework for the perfect fulfilment of the Gospel.

Here and there the reader will come across brief phrases which are epitomes of doctrine, usually more lapidary in the Latin than it is possible for them to be in English. Thus we read of the arriving guest: 'Every kindness should be shown him' (Ch. LIII, 'Exhibeatur ei omnis humanitas'); of daily work: 'Idleness is the enemy of the soul' (Ch. XLVIII); of prayer: 'Let it be short and pure unless drawn out by divine inspiration' (Ch. XX), or again on prayer: 'If someone wishes to pray, let him go in without hesitation and pray . . . with tears, and the attention of the heart' (Ch. LII); of the brotherhood: 'They should labour with chaste love at the charity of the brotherhood' (Ch. LXXII). One theme in particular should not go unmentioned: the Rule teaches us to recognise Christ in all persons and in all the circumstances of life: in the persons of the Abbot

(Ch. II), of the sick (Ch. XXXVI), of the poor (Ch. LIII), of the guest (Ch. LIII), and so on. And throughout there is an insistence that it is the disposition of the heart that counts rather than the external performance of the deed: this quality turns the Rule into a spiritual guide, as distinct from a set of laws.

The monks for whom the Rule legislated are not to be thought of as simply a gathering of local peasants. Monastic society was classless, but not therefore ignorant. Provision was made for manual work (Ch. XLVIII), but also arts and crafts (Ch. LVII) and a considerable period was allotted daily for spiritual reading ('lectio divina', Ch. XLVIII). A general distribution of books from the library is mentioned as taking place at the beginning of Lent, where thought is also given to those who are unable or unwilling to read, but they are thought of as exceptions (Ch. XLVIII). The normal equipment of the monk included a pen and writing materials. This basic provision for intellectual culture was to have a great development in later ages, and has even led to the impression that learning was a normal attribute of the Benedictine monk.

Thus the three main occupations of the monk's day were: the work of God (a time of mental as well as verbal prayer), the work of the hands (which in fact included all kinds of work) and spiritual reading (in which the mind was applied to study). These three occupations were seen as complementary; they exercised the monk at diverse levels—spiritual, intellectual and bodily, and so gave a balanced unity to each day.

One does not need to be a monk or a nun to find significance in the values of the Rule. There is a value of a society, set up as a stable and permanent unit, with a total indifference to gaining wealth or ease of living. There is the principle by which the individual fulfils himself through union with God, and on the social level, through love and service of his brethren. Ambition, greed, pride, domination, acquisitiveness are all proscribed and barriers laid down against them. It may seem a fearsome programme, but one which is worthy of consideration by a society which trains every individual to get to the top if he can, encourages all the 'haves' of society to acquire yet more, and leaves the co-ordination of its members to be settled by internal warfare. It is a society based on a totally opposite principle: 'By their fruits you shall know them' (Mt 7:20). Monasticism, as every other system run by men, has its failures, but at least it sheds light on the possibilities of a less egoistic society, suggests qualities necessary for social unity and success, and indicates what makes a path to social breakdown inevitable. Benedict himself lived in a time of social confusion and breakdown. No doubt this led him to a constant insistence on stability for his household. But it is not the sociological content that is his main message. That lies in the construction of a household based in its relationships on the divine teaching: 'Seek first his kingdom and its righteousness' (Mt 6:33). Whatever other merits the Rule may have flow from its concentration on that thought. This concentration is summed up at the conclusion of Ch. LXXII: 'They should prefer nothing to Christ. May he bring us all alike to life everlasting.'

*Note*
The traditional days of the year have been added in the margin for the benefit of any communities which may wish to use the text for reading aloud.

# INTRODUCTION

'Listen my son to the instructions of your Master, turn the ear of your heart to the advice of a loving father.'

These, the opening words of the Rule of St. Benedict, instantly capture our attention. These are the words of a loving father. Already Benedict has revealed his purpose: his Rule is all about love.

It is a practical guide to help men and women establish and maintain loving relationships with God, with others, with the material world, and also (perhaps surprisingly to those who associate Christianity, and in particular monasticism, with denial and asceticism) with one's own self. It is the whole person that is addressed in the Rule of St. Benedict. The whole God-given human being made up of body, mind and spirit. The Rule is written for a life which recognises that these three elements should be accepted and affirmed in a daily rhythm of prayer, study and work, alternating activities that make up that balanced life for which Benedictines are rightly renowned.

This balance, this *via media*, can be to some extent explained by Benedict's own life and character. Born around 480 in Nursia in Italy, in the years in which the Roman Empire and all its certainties were crumbling, he went to university in Rome but then fled in order to pursue the life of a hermit in a cave at Subiaco. Later he came to Monte Cassino where he founded a community of monks where he lived until his death in 547. Thus he knew from his own experiences both the life of a hermit and the life in community. He himself was both moderate and passionate. He wrote with *gravitas* and balance, as the last of the Romans, but he also brought the urgency of the charismatic preacher on fire with a message of fervent love.

The word Rule itself can sometimes be misleading to those unfamiliar with the spiritual realities of the Benedictine life. Benedict tells us to listen with 'the ear of your heart'. His concern in the Rule is always with the disposition of the heart itself. It is, as a contemporary Benedictine puts it, not a series of prescribed actions but a series of opening doors, an invitation to remain alert to the challenge of the Word itself.

'Who is the man who desires life and is eager to see Good Days?'

Right at the start of the Rule we are given a vivid picture of the Lord in the market place calling out to passers by with this offer of fullness of life (Prologue). Here is the possibility of a return, a change, a *metanoia*, for all those who have strayed 'through the slough of disobedience'. That way is bound to be narrow at the start but if we hold on with patience and perseverence, and above all with obedience, then the promise is that:

'through the continual practice of monastic observance and the life of faith, our hearts are opened wide, and the way of God's commandments is run in a sweetness of love that is beyond words' (Prologue).

When Benedict came to write his Rule there were already other monastic texts available, and many people were already living the monastic life. Basically people belonged to one of two groups. Either they were eremetical (seeking God in silence and solitude), or they were coenobetic (seeking God in the common life under the authority of an *abba*, a father). Modestly Benedict described his own effort as a little rule for beginners and

xviii

told his followers to read further in both these existing (and largely contradictory) traditions (Chapter 73).

But he was of course far too modest. For his compilation brings together the insights of both directions brilliantly and with such flexibility that for 1,500 years his Rule has continued to nurture and inspire men and women. It remains a spring or source to which both individuals and institutions can return time and again to find practical help and guidance, to be both reassured and challenged, to renew their vision.

Perhaps it is useful to see it as containing different levels of writing, a hierarchy of truths. There is the great ringing declaration of the Prologue, Chapter 72 with its panegyric on love, Chapter 7 with its profound exploration of humility, being earthed in the reality of self knowledge. But because it is also essentially a working document, legislation for the common shared life of a group of men (and we know from the Dialogues of St Gregory the Great AD 590-604, how disparate a group Benedict gathered around him at Monte Cassino) many of the chapters are concerned with minutiae which today make tedious, sometimes apparently irrelevant, reading. It is important to recognise this and see beyond it. It is in fact ironically just because it is so mundane and so concrete that the Rule continues to speak so forcibly.

Benedict does not deal in moral abstractions. Instead we are shown real life situations, the rota of kitchen servers (Chapter 35), the porter at the gate (Chapter 66) or the cellarer (bursar) handing out goods (Chapter 31). These confront us with the necessity of finding God, and practising love, in the ordinary, the commonplace, the unspectacular. It is precisely its specifity that makes the Rule so immediate and so inescapable. In its pages we see the radical demands of the Gospel in daily living.

Much of the Rule is taken up with practical discussions of the ordering of life. That is not because Benedict believed that good order is important for its own sake but because he knew that in a well ordered community it is easier to make space and time for God. When he declares that the oratory is the place set aside for prayer and should be used for nothing else (Chapter 52) he is establishing an important principle. He knows that certainty and a firm structure in externals provides a framework and a freedom, in which it becomes more possible to find a place for God. At the end of those chapters (8-18) which have dealt in considerable detail with the ordering of the Psalms he then says that if we can do better we are at liberty to try it (Chapter 18 V. 22). It is not the detail but the principle: muddle and confusion are to be avoided at all costs.

That offer of life in the Prologue comes from the Psalms (Psalm 33.12). It is, as is so much of the Rule, citation from Scripture. A quick glance at the text shows that there are in fact no less than 130 actual Biblical quotations within it. For Benedict is a man seized by the Word, shaped by it, his whole thought so totally formed by it that all he writes comes out of this deep knowledge and love of the Bible. Often the allusions are subtle, as when the cellarer is described as *non turbulentus* (not excitable) a reference to the suffering servant. Above all Benedict loves the Psalms and that is what he would wish for all who follow him. The saying of the daily offices centre on listening to the Word. This is the *opus dei*, the work of God, the life of prayer which is where the Rule is leading us. The corporate prayer is there to uphold a continuing awareness of the presence of God which makes praying inseparable from living, and living from praying.

Written as a guide for life in community, living at close quarters with other people, that most demanding of the human situations, Benedict takes as his starting point the worth of each and every person (Chapter 40). The Abbot handles everyone with a sensitivity that recognises the level at which they will develop to their full potential (Chapter 2). He is of course not only the exemplar of Christ to the brothers but also the example for each of us in our relations with others.

We are shown this in practice in all its ordinariness and dailiness, in the kitchen (Chapter 35) in the infirmary (Chapter 36), how the brothers quietly encourage one another as they get up (Chapter 22) and how lovingly they greet each other when they meet (Chapter 63). So finally when in Chapter 72 we are given that great exposition on love it only draws together all that has been explored earlier about the living out of love in day to day encounters.

The reverence and respect for persons is also found in the reverence and respect for material things. In fact the two are parallel: the job description for the cellarer, the man who handles the goods and property of the monastery is taken from the job description for a bishop (Chapter 31). Chapter 32 has much to say about the careful and responsible handling of tools entrusted to us, just as Chapter 4 lists the tools of the spiritual craft, and we must like faithful stewards return both in due time. For everything is on loan. When monks are told in Chapter 33 that they have nothing of their own that does not mean simply non-possession, it is more fundamental. It is their attitude that they consider nothing as private property. Here is a delicately crafted theology, in which the attitude towards our talents and possessions and towards people all inter- relate. This is one of Benedict's greatest gifts, for he is showing us the possibility of the totality and wholeness inherent in all of life.

Benedict's grasp of the human psyche, and his knowledge of the human predicament, is such that he speaks to all of us, his message is universal. When the novice on entering the community lays the three vows on the altar and says *Suscipe me (Accept me* Lord according to your word) that prayer and these vows reflect basic human needs. Stability is in essence a commitment to not trying to run away, to escape from the place in which one finds oneself; *conversatio morum* a commitment to continual conversion, to follow the call of Christ wherever it may lead; obedience, a commitment to hearing the voice of God and responding with a willing Yes.

These vows tell us much about ourselves on our journey to God, and about our relations with others; the need to stand firm but also to live open to change, and all the time to listen to God reaching out to us. But they also, like the whole Rule of St. Benedict itself, point us forwards towards the figure of Christ. Christ is the rock on whom we build. Christ is the way we follow. Christ is the word we hear.

'. . . prefer nothing whatever to Christ. May he bring us all alike to life everlasting' (Chapter 72).

This ultimately is the whole message of the Rule. It was a message that came through clearly to Benedict's own community, and it is a message that still comes through clearly to us today some 15 centuries later.

Esther de Waal

# The Rule of Saint Benedict

# Contents of The Rule of St Benedict

**Appendix**

**Epilogue**

# The Prologue

1 • Listen my son to the instructions of your Master, turn Jan. 1<br>May 2<br>Sept. 1 the ear of your heart to the advice of a loving father;

2 accept it willingly and carry it out vigorously; • so that through the toil of obedience you may return to him from whom you have separated by the sloth of disobedience.[1]

3 • To you, then, whoever you may be, are my words addressed, who, by the renunciation of your own will, are taking up the strong and glorious weapons of obedience in order to do battle in the service of the Lord Christ, the true King.

4 • First of all, whenever you begin any good work, you must ask of God with the most urgent prayer that it may

5 be brought to completion by him, • so that he, who has now deigned to reckon us in the number of his sons, may

6 not later on be made sad by our wicked actions. • For we must at all times use the good gifts he has placed in us, so that he will not later on disinherit us as an angry father

7 disinherits his sons; • nor like a feared lord, who has been roused to anger by our sins, hand over to eternal punishment us wicked slaves for refusing to follow him to glory.

8 • Let us then at last arouse ourselves, even as Jan. 2<br>May 3<br>Sept. 2 Scripture incites us in the words, 'Now is the hour for us

9 to rise from sleep.'[2] • Let us, then, open our eyes to the divine light, and hear with our ears the divine voice as it

10 cries out to us daily. • 'Today if you hear his voice, do not

11 harden your hearts,'[3] • and again, 'He who has ears to hear, let him hear what the Spirit says to the Churches.'[4]

12 • And what does the Spirit say? 'Come, my sons, listen to

---

[1] cf. Bar 4:28   [2] Rom 13:11   [3] Ps 94:8   [4] Rev 2:7

1

me; I shall teach you the fear of the Lord.'[5] • 'Run while 13 you have the light of life lest the darkness of death overwhelm you.'[6]

Jan. 3
May 4
Sept. 3
• And as the Lord seeks his workman in the mass of 14 people, he again cries out to him in the words, • 'Who is 15 the man who desires life and is eager to see Good Days?'[7] • If you hear this and reply, 'I do', God says to you, • 'If 16, 17 you want to have true and everlasting life, keep your tongue from speaking evil, and your lips from uttering deceit. Turn aside from evil and do good; seek peace and follow after it.'[8] • 'When you do this my eyes will be 18 upon you, and my ears will be open to your prayers, and before you call upon me I shall say to you: "Here I am".'[9] • What can be sweeter to us than this voice of the 19 Lord as he invites us, dearest brothers? • See how, in his 20 loving mercy, the Lord points out to us the Way of Life.[10]

Jan. 4
May 5
Sept. 4
• Let us therefore make for ourselves a girdle out of 21 faith and perseverance in good works, and under the guidance of the Gospel let us pursue our way in his paths, so that we may deserve to see him who has called us to his Kingdom. • For if we wish to make our home in 22 the dwelling-place of his Kingdom, there will be no getting there unless we run towards it by good deeds. • But let us question the Lord with the prophet, saying to 23 him, 'Lord, who shall make his home in your dwelling-place; who shall rest on your holy mountain?'[11] • And 24 then let us listen to the Lord's answer to our question, as he shows us the way to this dwelling-place, • saying, 'He 25 who walks without fault and does what is right; • he who 26 tells the truth in his heart; he who works no deceit with his tongue; • he who does no wrong to his neighbour; he 27

---

[5] Ps 33:13   [6] cf. Jn 12:35   [7] Ps 33:12   [8] ibid 14-15   [9] cf. Is 58:9   [10] Ps 25:10; Ac 9:2; 19:9, 23
[11] Ps 14:1

2

28 who does not slander his neighbour.'[12] • 'He who casts the wicked devil, even as he beguiles him, out of the sight of his heart, along with the temptation itself, and so reduces him to impotence, and takes the incipient thoughts that he suggests and dashes them against (the

29 rock of) Christ';[13] • those who fear the Lord and do not become conceited about keeping the law well, but realise that the good in themselves cannot be their own work but

30 is done by the Lord, • and who praise the Lord working within them, as they say with the prophet, 'Not unto us, Lord, not unto us, but unto your name, give the

31 glory.'[14] • For neither did the Apostle Paul give himself any credit for his preaching, but said, 'By the grace of

32 God I am what I am.'[15] • And the same Apostle also said, 'He who boasts must boast in the Lord.'[16]

33 • And so the Lord also says in the Gospel, 'Everyone who listens to these words of mine and acts on them, will be like a sensible man who built his house on rock;

34 • floods rose, gales blew and hurled themselves against that house, and it did not fall; it was founded on rock.'[17]

35 • Thus the Lord concludes his reply, and daily expects us to respond through our dutiful actions to his holy precepts.

36 • Therefore in order that amends may be made for sins, the days of our life are prolonged to give us a time

37 in which to make our piece, • as the Apostle says, 'Do you realise that the patience of God is meant to lead you

38 to repentance?'[18] • For this loving Lord says, 'I do not wish the death of the sinner, but that he should change his ways and live.'[19]

39 • We have asked the Lord, my brothers, about the

Jan. 5
May 6
Sept. 5

Jan. 6
May 7
Sept. 6

---

[12] Ps 2,3   [13] Ps 136:9   [14] Ps 113:1   [15] 1 Co 15:10   [16] II Co 10:17   [17] Mt 7:25   [18] Rm 2:4
[19] Ezk 33:11

3

kind of man who dwells in his house, and we have heard what is required in order to do so. So let us fulfil the task of such a dweller. • That means that we must make 40 ready our hearts and bodies to engage in the warfare of holy obedience to his commands, • and because our 41 nature has not power to do this, we must ask God to send forth the help of his grace to our aid. • And, if we wish to 42 escape the punishment of hell and reach eternal life, • then while there is still time, while we are still living in 43 this body and this life gives us the light to do all these things, • we must hurry to do now what will profit us for 44 ever.

Jan. 7
May 8
Sept. 7 • We propose, therefore to establish a school of the 45 Lord's service, • and in setting it up we hope we shall lay 46 down nothing that is harsh or hard to bear. • But if for 47 adequate reason, for the correction of faults or the preservation of charity, some degree of restraint is laid down, • do not then and there be overcome with terror, 48 and run away from the way of salvation, for its beginning must needs be difficult.[20] • On the contrary, through the 49 continual practice of monastic observance and the life of faith, our hearts are opened wide, and the way of God's commandments is run in a sweetness of love that is beyond words. • Let us then never withdraw from 50 discipleship to him, but persevering in his teachings in the monastery till death, let us share the sufferings of Christ through patience, and so deserve also to share in his kingdom.

[20] Mt 7:14

4

# Preliminary Survey

# Chapter I The Kinds of Monk

Jan. 8
May 9
Sept. 8

1 • It is clear that there are four kinds of monk.

2 • The first kind are the Cenobites, that is the 'monastery' kind, who do battle under a Rule and an Abbot.

3 • Then the second kind are the Anchorites or Hermits; these are they who are no longer in the first fervour of their religious life but have been tested for a long time in

4 the monastery • and have learnt, with the assistance of

5 many brothers, how to do battle against the devil. • and now, well equipped to leave the fraternal battle-line for the solitary combat of the desert, they are strong enough to do battle against the vices of the body and the mind on their own, with their own resources, relying on God's aid, but now without the support of anyone else.

Jan. 9
May 10
Sept. 9

6 • The third kind of monk is the abominable one of Sarabaites, who have not been tested by a rule, as gold is tested in a furnace, nor been taught by experience, but

7 are like soft lead. • They keep faith with this world by their actions, but manifestly lie to God by their tonsure.

8 • These people live in twos and threes, or even alone; they have no shepherd, they shut themselves up in their own sheepfolds, not those of the Lord; and their law

9 consists in yielding to their desires: • what they like or choose they call holy, and they reckon illicit whatever displeased them.

10 • The fourth kind of monk are those called Wanderers. These are never stable throughout their whole lives but wanderers through diverse regions, receiving hospitality in the monastic cells of others for three or four days at a

11 time. • Always roving and never settling, they follow

7

their own wills, enslaved by the attractions of gluttony. They are in all respects worse than the Sarabaites.

• It is better to pass over in silence than to speak 12 further of the unhappy way of life of all these people, • so 13 let us pass them by, and with God's help set about organising the strongest kind of monks — the Cenobites.

# 1
# The Formation and Nature of the Monastery

# Chapter II What Kind of Man the Abbot should be

1 • An Abbot who is worthy to be in charge of a monastery must always bear in mind what he is called and fulfil in Jan. 10 May 11 Sept. 10
2 his actions the name of one who is called greater.[1] • For he is believed to act in the place of Christ in the
3 monastery, since he is called by his title, • as the Apostle says, 'You have received the Spirit of adoption as sons,
4 through whom we cry, Abba! Father!'[2] • Therefore the Abbot should not teach or ordain or command anything
5 that lies outside the Lord's commands, far from it; • but his commands and his teaching should mingle like the leaven of divine justice in the mind of his disciples.
6 • The Abbot must always remember that at the fearful judgement of God two things will be discussed: his own
7 teaching and the obedience of his disciples. • The Abbot must also realise that whatever lack of fruitfulness the Father of the family may find in his sheep will be blamed
8 on the shepherd. • And likewise if the shepherd has laboured with complete diligence over a troublesome and disobedient flock, and has expended every care over their
9 diseased behaviour, • he will be acquitted in the Lord's judgement and will say with the prophet, 'I have not hidden your justice in my heart, but I have spoken of your truth and saving help';[3] 'but they have contemp-
10 tuously despised me.'[4] • And then finally the penalty of death will swallow up the sheep who were disobedient to his care.
11 • When, therefore, anyone takes the name of Abbot, he should rule over his disciples with two kinds of teaching; Jan. 11 May 12 Sept. 11
12 • that is to say, he must show forth all good and holy

---

[1] Mt 18:4  [2] Rm 8:15  [3] Ps 39:11  [4] Is 1:2

things by his words and even more by his deeds. To apt disciples he must explain the Lord's teaching by word, but to those who are hard of heart or simple of mind he must make clear the divine teaching by his actions. • By 13 his deeds he must make it clear that nothing may be done which he has taught his disciples to be forbidden, lest while he preaches to others he should merit rejection himself, • and God should some day say to him as he 14 sins, 'What business have you reciting my statutes, standing there mouthing my covenant, since you detest my discipline, and thrust my words behind you?'[5] • And 15 'you observed the splinter in your brother's eye, and did not notice the plank in your own?'[6]

Jan. 12
May 13
Sept. 12 • The Abbot must not show personal preferences in his 16 monastery. • He must not be more loving to one than to 17 another, unless he had found him to be more advanced in good works or in obedience. • A free-born man must not 18 be put before one entering the monastery from slavery, unless some other reasonable cause exists. • But if it 19 seems to the Abbot that there is good reason for it, let him do so, and let him do the same about the rank of anyone. Otherwise let them keep their normal order. • For whether we are slaves or freemen, we are all one in 20 Christ, and serve on equal terms in the army of one Lord; 'for God has no favourites.'[7] • In regard to rank we find 21 distinction in his eyes only if we are found humble and better than others in good works. • Therefore the Abbot 22 should show himself equally loving to all, and maintain discipline impartially according to the merits of each.

Jan. 13
May 14
Sept. 13 • In his teaching the Abbot should always observe the 23 method of the Apostle, 'Employ arguments, appeals and rebukes.'[8] • He must behave differently at different 24

---

[5] Ps 49:16, 17   [6] Mt 7:3   [7] Rm 2:11   [8] II Tm 4:2

12

times, sometimes using threats, sometimes encouragement. He must show the tough attitude of a master, and
25 also the loving affection of a father. • Thus he should sternly reprimand the undisciplined and unruly, but entreat the obedient, the meek and the patient to go forward in virtue; as for the careless and the scornful,
26 we instruct him to rebuke and correct them. • He should not pretend that he does not see the faults of offenders, but remember the danger overhanging Eli, priest of Shiloh and, as best he can, he should cut them out by the
27 roots as soon as they begin to show themselves. • He should correct upright and intelligent minds with verbal
28 admonitions once or twice, • but the shameless, the thick-skinned and the proud or disobedient, he should repress at the very beginning of their sinful ways with the corporal punishment of blows, bearing in mind what is
29 written, 'The fool is not corrected by words,'[9] • and again, 'Strike your son with the rod and you will deliver his soul from death.'[10]

30 • The Abbot should always bear in mind what he is;
31 he should bear in mind what he is called; • and let him realise that more is demanded of him to whom more is entrusted. He must realise also how difficult and arduous is the task he has undertaken, that of ruling souls and serving men of many different characters; one, indeed, to be encouraged, another to be rebuked, another
32 persuaded, • each according to his nature and intelligence. Thus he must adapt and fit himself to all, so that not only will he not lose any of the flock entrusted to him, but he will rejoice as his good flock increases.

33 • It is most important that he should not pay greater attention to transient earthly things that pass away, and

Jan. 14
May 15
Sept. 14

Jan. 15
May 16
Sept. 15

---

[9] cf. Pr 19:29   [10] cf. Pr 19:18; 23:14

13

so fail to recognise or underestimate the salvation of the souls entrusted to him. • Let him always consider that it 34 is souls that he has undertaken to rule, and for whom he will give an account. • Moreover, in order that he may 35 not complain of reduced temporal goods, let him remember the Scripture, 'Seek God's Kingdom first, and his righteousness, and all these other things will be given you as well,'[11] • and again, 'Nothing is lacking to those 36 who fear him.'[12] • Let him realise that he who under- 37 takes to rule souls must prepare himself to give an account. • Whatever the number of brethren under his 38 care, he must understand clearly that he will have to render an account on the Day of Judgement for all these souls, in addition, of course, to his own. • Thus as he 39 bears ever in mind the enquiry that will be made on the shepherd's care of the sheep entrusted to him, the thought that he takes concerning the accounts to be rendered for others will make him careful of his own state. • And so, while he provides by his instructions for 40 the amendment of others, he will be brought also to the amendment of his own faults.

[11] Mt 7:33    [12] Ps 33:10

# Chapter III On summoning the Brethren to Council

1 • Whenever anything important has to be done in the monastery the Abbot must assemble the whole com-
2 munity and explain what is under consideration. • When he had heard the counsel of the brethren, he should give it consideration and then take what seems to him the best
3 course. • The reason why we say that all should be called to council is this: It is often to a younger brother that the
4 Lord reveals the best course. • But the brethren must give their counsel submissively and humbly and not
5 presume stubbornly to defend their opinions. • The decision should, however, depend mainly on the Abbot's judgement, and all should be joined in obedience to what
6 he considers the soundest course. • But just as it is fitting that disciples should obey their master, so it is incumbent on him to settle everything with foresight and justice.

Jan. 16
May 17
Sept. 16

7 • In every circumstance, therefore, all should follow the authority of the Rule, nor is it to be rashly abandoned
8 by anyone. • No one in the monastery is to follow the
9 prompting of his own heart; • no one is to presume to argue rudely with the Abbot, or to argue at all outside
10 the monastery. • If anyone does so presume, he must
11 submit to disciplinary measures. • The Abbot himself, however, in all his actions must fear God and keep the Rule, bearing in mind that most surely he will have to render account for all his decisions before God, the most just judge.

Jan. 17
May 18
Sept. 17

12 • If, however, there are less important matters to be transacted for the well-being of the monastery, the Abbot
13 should take counsel only with the senior monks, • for it is

written, 'Take counsel about all you do and afterwards you will have no regrets.'[1]

---

[1] Sir 32:19

# Chapter IV The Tools of Good Works

1 • In the first place to love the Lord God with all one's heart, with all one's soul and with all one's strength.[1] Jan. 18 May 19 Sept. 18

2 • Then to love one's neighbour as oneself[2]

3 • Then not to kill

4 • Not to commit adultery

5 • Not to steal

6 • Not to covet

7 • Not to bear false witness

8 • To honour all men[3]

9 • Not to do to another what one would not wish to have done to oneself

10 • To deny oneself in order to follow Christ

11 • To punish one's body

12 • Not to seek pleasures

13 • To love fasting

14 • To relieve the poor

15 • To clothe the naked

16 • To visit the sick

17 • To bury the dead

18 • To give help in trouble

19 • To console the sorrowful

20 • To avoid worldly behaviour

21 • To set nothing before the love of Christ

22 • Not to give way to anger Jan. 19 May 20 Sept. 19

23 • Not to cherish an opportunity for displaying one's anger

24 • Not to preserve deceit in one's heart

25 • Not to give the kiss of peace insincerely

26 • Not to abandon charity

---

[1] Mt 22:37   [2] ibid. 39   [3] 1 P 2:17

- Not to swear, for fear of perjury 27
- To speak with one's mouth the truth that lies in one's 28
heart
- Not to return evil for evil 29
- Not to inflict any injury, but to suffer injuries patiently 30
- To love one's enemies[4] 31
- Not to curse anyone who curses us, but instead to 32
return a blessing
- To suffer persecution for righteousness' sake 33
- Not to be arrogant 34
- Not given to drinking 35
- Not a heavy eater 36
- Not given to much sleeping 37
- Not lazy 38
- Not a grumbler 39
- Not a detractor 40
- To rest one's hope in God 41
- Whenever one perceives any good in oneself to 42
attribute it to God, not to one's self
- But to recognise that whatever is evil is one's own 43
doing, and to blame one's self

Jan. 20
May 21
Sept. 20 - To fear the Day of Judgement[5] 44
- To dread hell 45
- To yearn for eternal life with all possible spiritual 46
desire
- *To keep death daily before one's eyes* 47
- At every moment to keep watch over the actions of 48
one's life
- In every place to know that God most surely beholds 49
one
- To dash the evil thoughts that invade one's heart 50
immediately upon Christ, as upon a rock, and to reveal

---

[4] Mt 5:43   [5] Mt 10:28

18

them to one's spiritual father
51 • To guard one's mouth against evil and vicious speech
52 • Not to love much talking
53 • Not to utter words that are foolish and provoke laughter
54 • Not to love much or unrestrained laughter
55 • To listen willingly to devout reading
56 • To fall often to prayer
57 • In our daily prayer to God to confess with tears and groans the wrong-doing in our past life
58 • To amend these wrong ways in the future
59 • To reject carnal desires
60 • To hate one's own will
61 • To obey the Abbot's commands in everything, even though he himself (which God forbid) acts otherwise, remembering always that command of the Lord's, 'Do what they tell you, but do not do the things that they do'[6]
62 • To be unwilling to be called holy before one is so, but to be holy first so that it may be truly said of one
63 • To carry out God's commands daily in one's actions
64 • To love chastity
65 • To hate no one
66 • Not to cherish bitterness
67 • Not to indulge in envy
68 • Not to love quarelling
69 • To flee vainglory
70 • To revere the elders
71 • To love the young
72 • To pray for one's enemies in the love of Christ
73 • After a quarrel to make peace with the other before sunset
74 • And never to despair of God's mercy

Jan. 21
May 22
Sept. 21

[6] Mt 23:3

• These then are the tools of the spiritual craft. • If we 75, 76
make full use of them unceasingly day and night, then,
when we give them back on the Day of Judgement, we
shall in return receive from the Lord that reward which
he himself has promised, • 'The things that no eye had 77
seen, and no ear has heard, which God has prepared for
those who love him.'[7] • Now the workshop in which we 78
make diligent use of all these tools is the enclosure of the
monastery combined with stability in the community.

---

[7] I Co 2:9

# Chapter V Obedience

1,2 • The first step in humility is prompt obedience. • This is fitting for those who hold nothing more dear to them 3 than Christ. • Because they had made profession of holy service or for fear of hell or to attain the glory of 4 everlasting life, • immediately when something has been commanded by a superior, it is for them as a divine command and they cannot allow any delay in its 5 execution. • The Lord says of them, 'As soon as he heard 6 me, he obeyed me.'[1] • And he said also to those who are to teach, 'Whoever listens to you listens to me.'[2]

7 • Such men, therefore, at once leave whatever they are 8 engaged on, abandon their own will, • and with hands set free by leaving unfinished what they are doing, with the quick feet of obedience, follow by action the voice of 9 him who gives the order. • And so it is as if in a single moment the order of the master is uttered and the work of the disciple is completed with the speed inspired by the fear of the Lord. The two things are swiftly 10 completed together • by those in whose hearts lies the 11 desire of reaching eternal life. • Thus they take the narrow way, as the Lord says, 'Narrow is the way that 12 leads to life.'[3] • So they do not live according to their own wills, nor obey their own desires and pleasures, but behaving in accordance with the rule and judgement of another, they live in monasteries and desire to have an 13 Abbot ruling over them. • Without doubt such men imitate the mind of the Lord in his saying, 'I came to do not my own will, but that of him who sent me.'[4]

14 • This obedience of which we speak will be acceptable

---

[1] Ps 17:44  [2] Lk 10:16  [3] Mt 7:14  [4] Jn 6:38

to God and agreeable to men if what is ordered is carried out without fearfulness, without slowness in performance, without half-heartedness or grumbling or an unwilling reply. • For the obedience that is shown to superiors is 15 shown to God; for he said himself, 'He who listens to you, listens to me.'[5] • And it should be offered by the disciples 16 with good will, because 'God loves a cheerful giver.'[6] • For if a disciple obeys grudgingly, if he complains not 17 only in words but even in thought, • then, although he 18 carries out the order it will not now be acceptable to God, who sees that his heart is grumbling; • and for work 19 like this he will get no reward—indeed, he incurs the penalty for grumblers, unless he make amends with penance.

---

[5] Lk 10:16    [6] II Co 9:7

# Chapter VI On keeping silent

1 • Let us do what the prophet says, 'I have resolved: I will watch how I behave and not let my tongue lead me into sin; I set a muzzle over my mouth; I stayed dumb, I was humbled, I refrained from speaking even good words.'[1] Jan. 24 May 25 Sept. 24
2 • Here the prophet teaches that if we should sometimes for the sake of the virtue of silence refrain even from good conversation, we should all the more, for fear of the penalty of sin, refrain from evil words. 3 • Therefore, because of the great importance of keeping silence, permission to speak should be rarely given even to exemplary disciples, for conversation that is good and holy and edifying; 4 • for it is written, 'If you talk a lot you 5 will not escape falling into sin,'[2] • and elsewhere, 'Death 6 and life are in the power of the tongue.'[3] • Indeed it is fitting for the master to speak and teach; the disciple's part is to keep silent and to listen.

7 • Therefore, if it is necessary to ask a superior for something, the request should be made with humility 8 and submissive reverence. • But as for loose talk, idle words and talk that stimulates laughter, we condemn this with a permanent ban in all places, and we do not allow a disciple to open his mouth in this kind of speech.

---

[1] Ps 38:2, 3  [2] Pr 10:19  [3] Pr 18:21

# Chapter VII Humility

Jan. 25
May 26
Sept. 25
• Brothers, Holy Scripture cries aloud to us, saying, 1
'Whoever exalts himself will be humbled, and he who
humbles himself will be exalted.'[1] • When it says this it is 2
teaching that all exaltation is a kind of pride. • And the 3
prophet shows that he himself was on his guard against
it, when he said, 'Lord, my heart has no lofty ambitions,
my eyes do not look too high; I am not concerned with
great affairs, or marvels beyond my scope.'[2] • Why thus? 4
'If I did not think humbly, but exalted my soul, as a child
on the mother's breast is weaned, so did you treat my
soul.'[3]

Jan. 26
May 27
Sept. 26
• So, brothers, if we wish to reach the highest peak of 5
humility, and to arrive quickly at that state of heavenly
exaltation which is attained in the present life through
humility, • then that ladder which appeared to Jacob in 6
his dream, on which he saw angels going up and down,
must be set up, so that we may mount by our own
actions. • Certainly that going down and up is to be 7
understood by us in the sense that we go down through
pride and up through humility. • The ladder itself that is 8
set up is our life in this world, and the setting up is
effected by the Lord in the humbled heart. • The sides of 9
the ladder we call the body and soul, and in them the
divine call inserts the diverse rungs of humility and
(interior) discipline.

Jan. 27
May 28
Sept. 27
• The first step of humility, then, is for a man to set the 10
fear of God always before his eyes, and utterly to avoid
forgetfulness. • He must always remember all God's 11
commandments, and constantly turn over in his heart

---

[1] Lk 18:14  [2] Ps 130:1  [3] ibid. 2

how hell will burn those who despise him by their sins, and how eternal life has been prepared for those who fear
12 him. • At every moment a man must be on his guard against sins and vices—vices of thought, word, hand, foot or self-will, and also against the desires of the flesh.
13 • He must recognise that he is at every hour in the sight of God in heaven, and that his actions are everywhere visible to the divine eyes of God, and are being reported
14 to God by the angels from moment to moment. • This is made clear to us by the prophet when he shows us that God is always present in our thoughts, 'God examines',
15 he says, 'the heart and the mind.'[4] • And also, 'The Lord
16 knows exactly how men think.'[5] • And yet again, 'You
17 read my thoughts from far away'[6] • and 'Even the
18 thought of man shall praise you.'[7] • In order then to keep his perverse thoughts under careful control, the profitable brother should repeat in his heart, 'Then I shall be spotless in his sight, if I keep myself in check against my sinfulness.'[8]

19 • Scripture, indeed, forbids us to do our own will,
20 saying to us, 'Turn away from your will.'[9] • Moreover, we ask God in our prayers that his will may be done in
21 us. • Truly then we are taught not to do our own will, when we accept the warning of Scripture, 'There are ways which seem right to a man, but in the end they
22 plunge him into the depth of hell,'[10] • and also when we tremble at what is said of the indifferent, 'They are
23 corrupt and depraved in their pleasures.'[11] • Indeed in what concerns the desires of the flesh, we must believe that God is ever present to us, even as the prophet says, 'All my desires are known to you.'[12]

Jan. 28
May 29
Sept. 28

---

[4] Ps 7:10   [5] Ps 93:11   [6] Ps 138:3   [7] Ps 75:11   [8] Ps 17:24   [9] Sir 18:30   [10] Pr 16:25
[11] Ps 13:1   [12] Ps 37:10

Jan. 29
May 30
Sept. 29
• We must, therefore, be on our guard against any evil 24
desire, because death is stationed beside the entrance to
delight, • as Scripture teaches in the words, 'Do not go 25
after your lusts.'[13] • So if the eyes of the Lord are upon 26
the good and the wicked[14] • and if the Lord is always 27
looking down from heaven upon the children of men to
see if there are any that act wisely and seek after God,[15]
• and if daily our works are reported to the Lord by the 28
angels assigned to us, then brethren, • we must constantly 29
be on our guard, lest one day God beholds us falling into
sin and becoming unprofitable • and (although he spare 30
us in this life because he is merciful and waits for our
repentance) he should say to us in the hereafter, 'This
you did, and I was silent.'[16]

Jan. 30
May 31
Sept. 30
• The second step of humility is that a man should not 31
love his own will nor take pleasure in carrying out his
desires, • but rather by his actions imitate the Lord in his 32
saying, 'I came not to do my own will, but that of him
who sent me.'[17] • And it has been written, 'Self- 33
indulgence brings its penalty, endurance brings forth a
crown.'

Jan. 31
June 1
Oct. 1
• The third step of humility is that for the love of God 34
one should be obedient to a superior in all things,
imitating the Lord of whom the Apostle says, 'He was
made obedient even unto death.'[18]

Feb. 1
June 2
Oct. 2
• The fourth step of humility is that, when in the very 35
act of obeying one meets with trials, opposition, and even
abuse, a man should, with an uncomplaining spirit, keep
a firm grip on patience • and as he endures he should 36
neither grow faint nor run away; even as Scripture says,
'He who stands firm to the end will be saved,'[19] • and 37

---

[13] Sir 18:30   [14] Pr 15:3   [15] Ps 13:2   [16] Ps 49:21   [17] Jn 6:38   [18] Ph 2:8
[19] Mt 10:22

26

again, 'Let your heart take courage and hope in the
38 Lord.'[20] • Further, to show us how a faithful man should
suffer all things, however painful, on the Lord's behalf, it
gives voice to those who suffer in the words, 'For your
sake we are afflicted by death all the day long, and are
39 reckoned as sheep for slaughter.'[21] • Yet unmoved,
through their hope of divine reward they joyfully
persevere, saying, 'These are the trials through which
40 we triumph on account of him who has loved us.'[22] • And
elsewhere Scripture says again, 'You tested us, O God;
you refined us in the fire as silver is refined; you led us
41 into the net; you laid tribulations on our backs'[23] • And
to show that we ought to be under a superior, it
continues, 'You have set men over our heads.'[24]
42 • Precisely then they patiently fulfil the command of the
Lord in these trials and rebuffs, and when they are struck
on one cheek they offer the other.[25] When someone takes
away their tunic they allow him to take their cloak also.
43 When they are forced to go one mile, they go two; • like
the Apostle Paul they put up with false brethren, and bless
those who curse them.[26]

44 • The fifth step of humility is that a man should in
humble confession reveal to his Abbot all the evil
thoughts that come into his mind, and any wrongful
45 actions that he had done in secret. • In this connection
Scripture exhorts us in the words, 'Reveal your course to
46 the Lord, and hope in him,'[27] • and again, 'Make
confession to the Lord for he is good, and his mercy is
47 everlasting;'[28] • and yet again the prophet says, 'I have
declared my sin to you, I have not covered up my evil
48 actions; • I made this resolve: I will confess my evil deeds

Feb. 2
June 3
Oct. 3

---

[20] Ps 26:14   [21] Rm 8:36   [22] ibid. 37   [23] Ps 65: 10, 11   [24] ibid. 12   [25] Mt 5:39-41
[26] I Co 4:12   [27] Ps 36:5   [28] Ps 105:1

27

to the Lord, and you have forgiven the guilt of my heart.'[29]

Feb. 3
June 4
Oct. 4 • The sixth step of humility is that a monk should be 49 satisfied with whatever is of lowest value or quality, and with regard to the tasks laid on him should think of himself as a bad and unworthy workman, • repeating to 50 himself the words of the prophet, 'I have been brought to nothing; I have known nothing; I am like a pack-animal before you . . . and yet I am always with you.'[30]

Feb. 4
June 5
Oct. 5 • The seventh step of humility is that he should not 51 only say in words that he is inferior and less virtuous than all other men, but that he should really believe it in the depth of his heart, • making the same act of humility 52 as the prophet, who says, 'I am a worm and no man; the scorn of mankind, the jest of the people.'[31] • 'I have been 53 lifted up, I have been brought down, and reduced to confusion.'[32] • And again, 'It is good for me that you 54 have humiliated me, so that I may learn your commandments.'[33]

Feb. 5
June 6
Oct. 6 • The eighth step of humility is that a monk should do 55 nothing except what is recommended by the common rule of the monastery and the example of those above

Feb. 6
June 7
Oct. 7 him. 56

•The ninth step of humility is that a monk should keep his tongue from talking; he should preserve silence and 57 not speak until he is questioned, • for the Scripture teaches that, 'In much talking, one will not escape sin,'[34] 58 • and that 'the talkative man is not directed in his life.'[35]

Feb. 7
June 8
Oct. 8 • The tenth step of humility is that he should not be 59 ready and quick to laughter, for it is written, 'The fool raises his voice in laughter.'[36]

---

[29] Ps 31:5   [30] Ps 73:22, 23   [31] Ps 21:7   [32] Ps 87:16   [33] Ps 118:71   [34] Pr 10:19   [35] Ps 139:12
[36] Sir 21:23

28

60     • The eleventh step of humility is that when a monk speaks, he does so quietly, without laughter, with humility, with restraint, making use of few words and 61 reasonable ones, • as it is written, 'The wise man becomes known for his few words.'

Feb. 8
June 9
Oct. 9

62     • The twelfth step of humility is not only that a monk should be humble of heart, but also that in his appearance his humility should be apparent to those who see him.

Feb. 9
Ju·e 10
Oct. 10

63     • That is to say: whether he is at the work of God, in the oratory, in the monastery, in the garden, on the road, in the field or anywhere else, whether sitting, walking or standing, he should always have his head bowed, his eyes 64 fixed on the ground, • and should at every moment be considering his guilt for his sins and thinking that he is 65 even now being presented for the dread judgement. • He should always be saying in his heart what the tax-gatherer in the Gospel said with downcast eyes, 'Lord, sinner as I am, I am not worthy to raise my eyes to 66 heaven;'[37] • or again with the prophet, 'I am bowed down and humbled at all times.'[38]

67     • Thus when all these steps of humility have been climbed, the monk will soon reach that love of God 68 which, being perfect, drives out all fear.[39] • Through this love all the practices which before he kept somewhat fearfully, he now begins to keep effortlessly and naturally 69 and habitually, • influenced now not by any fear of hell but by the force of long practice, and the very delight he 70 experiences in virtue. • These things the Lord, working through his Holy Spirit, will deign to show in his workman, when he has been purified from vice and sin.

---

[37] cf. Lk 18:13    [38] Ps 118:107    [39] I Jn 4:18

Feb. 10
June 11
Oct. 11

• Having considered what is reasonable we lay down 1 that during the winter (that is from 1 November till Easter) the time of rising will be the eighth hour of the night. • Thus they may sleep for a while after midnight 2 and get up after digestion has been completed. • The 3 time that is left after Matins is to be used for further study by the brethren whose knowledge of the Psalter or of the readings is incomplete. • From Easter till the 4 aforesaid 1 November, the hour of rising should be so determined that there is a short interval after Matins, during which the brethren can go out for the necessities of nature. Lauds which follow are to be said as dawn is breaking.

# Chapter IX The Number of Psalms to be said at the Night Office

1 • During the winter period mentioned above, first of all
there should be said three times the versicle, 'Lord open
2 my lips, and my mouth will proclaim your praise,'[1] • to
3 be followed by Psalm 3 and the *Glory be*; • after this
Psalm 94 should be chanted with an antiphon, or at least
4 chanted. • Then the hymn should follow, and next, six
5 Psalms with antiphons. • When these are ended and the
versicle has been said, the Abbot should pronounce a
blessing. Then when all are seated in their stalls, three
readings should be read by the brethren in turn from the
book on the lectern, and between them three responsories
6 should be sung. • Two responsories should be sung
without the *Glory be*, but after the third reading, the
7 singer should chant the *Glory be*, • and when he begins it
all should at once rise from their seats in honour and
8 reverence for the Holy Trinity. • The books of divine
authorship, of both the Old and New Testaments, should
be read at Matins, and also the commentaries on them
written by well-known and approved Catholic Fathers.
9 • After these readings with their responsories another six
Psalms should follow; they are to be sung with Alleluia.
10 • After these Psalms, there should follow a reading from
the Apostle, recited by heart, the versicle, and the prayer
11 of the litany, that is *Lord have mercy*. • And so let Matins
conclude.

Feb. 11
June 12
Oct. 12

[1] Ps 50:17

31

# Chapter X How the Praise of God is to be performed on Summer Nights

Feb. 12
June 13
Oct. 13

• From Easter till November the same number of Psalms, as set down above, is to be retained, • but on account of the nights being short, no lessons are to be read from the book. Instead of these three readings, one from the Old Testament is to be recited by heart, followed by a short responsory. • All the rest should be carried out as set down above. Thus, never less than twelve Psalms should be said at Matins, not counting the 3rd and 94th.

# Chapter XI How Matins are to be carried out on Sundays

Feb. 13
June 14
Oct. 14

1 • On Sundays the hour of rising for Matins should be
2 earlier. • In this Office the method is as follows. When
the six Psalms and the versicle have been chanted, as we
set out above, and all are seated in due order in their
stalls, four readings should be read from the book (as we
3 said before) with their responsories, • and the *Glory be* is
chanted only in the fourth responsory. When he begins it
4 all should rise at once with reverence. • After these
readings another six Psalms should follow in order with
5 antiphons, as before, and a versicle. • After these again
four more lessons should be read with responsories, as set
6 out before. • Then three canticles from the prophets, as
chosen by the Abbot, should be sung with Alleluia.
7 • When the verse has been said, the Abbot gives a
blessing, and four more lessons are read from the New
8 Testament in the way already described. • After the
fourth responsory the Abbot intones the hymn *We praise*
9 *you, O God;* • when this is finished the Abbot reads from
10 the Gospel, while all stand in reverential honour. • At
the end of the reading all reply *Amen*, and then the Abbot
begins the hymn *To You Praise is due*, and after the prayer,
11 they begin Lauds. • This order of Matins is to be kept on
12 Sundays in both the summer and winter seasons— •
unless by chance they get up late (which should not
happen) and some abridgement of the readings or
13 responsories has to be made. • But great care should be
taken that this does not happen, but if it does, the person
through whose carelessness it has occurred must make
adequate satisfaction to God in the oratory.

# Chapter XII How the Solemn Office of Lauds is to be carried out

Feb. 14
June 15
Oct. 15 • Lauds on Sunday begin with Psalm 66, chanted 1 continuously without an antiphon. • After that, Psalm 50 2 is chanted with Alleluia. • And then Psalm 117 and 3 Psalm 62. • Then the canticle *O All you Works of the Lord,* 4 *Bless the Lord,* and the *Praises,*[1] a reading from the Apocalypse learnt by heart, a responsory, the hymn, the versicle, the canticle from the Gospels, and the litany to form the conclusion.

---

[1] Psalms 148-50

# Chapter XIII How Lauds are carried out on ordinary Days

1 • On ordinary days the solemn Office of Lauds is to be
2 carried out as follows: • Psalm 66 is to be said without an
antiphon, and rather slowly (as on Sunday) so that all
may arrive in time for Psalm 50 which is to be chanted
3 with an antiphon. • After this, let two more Psalms be
4 chanted, keeping to custom, namely: • on Monday 5 and
5,6 35, • on Tuesday 42 and 56, • on Wednesday 63 and 64,
7,8,9 • on Thursday 87 and 89, • on Friday 75 and 91, • and
on Saturday 142, and the canticle of Deuteronomy,
10 divided into two parts. • On each of the other days is
sung a canticle from the prophets, as in the Roman
11 Church. • The *Praises* follow, and then a single reading
from the Apostle to be recited by heart, the responsory,
hymn, verse, canticle from the Gospels, and the litany to
form the end.

12 • Definitely neither Lauds nor Vespers should finish
without the Lord's Prayer being recited at the end by the
superior, while all listen. This is on account of the thorns
of mutual offence which occur in the course of events;
13 • for in this way they are warned by the undertaking
contained in the words of the prayer, *Forgive us as we
forgive* and may cleanse their hearts from any defect of
14 this kind. • In the other Offices only the last part of this
prayer is said, so that all may reply, *But deliver us from evil.*

Feb. 15
June 16
Oct. 16

Feb. 16
June 17
Oct. 17

# Chapter XIV How Matins are carried out on Feast Days of Saints

Feb. 17
June 18
Oct. 18

• On the feasts of saints and on all solemn days Matins 1 are to be carried out as we have laid down for Sundays, • except that the Psalms, antiphons and readings proper 2 to the day should be said; but the order of the Office should be as previously detailed.

# Chapter XV When Alleluia is to be said

1 • From the holy feast of Easter until Pentecost Alleluia should be said throughout the Office both in the Psalms and in the responses. Feb. 18<br>June 19<br>Oct. 19

2 • From Pentecost till the beginning of Lent it should be said every night with the second group of Psalms only.

3 • On every Sunday (outside Lent) the canticles of Matins, Lauds, Prime, Terce, Sext and None should be said with Alleluia; but Vespers should be sung with an antiphon.

4 • Except from Easter to Pentecost, responsories are never to be said with Alleluia.

# Chapter XVI How the Work of God is carried out during the Daytime

Feb. 19
June 20
Oct. 20
• As the prophet puts it, 'Seven times daily I have [1]
praised you.'[1] • This sacred number of seven will be [2]
performed by us if we carry out the duties of our service
at Lauds, Prime, Terce, Sext, None, Vespers and
Compline, • for it is of these hours of the day that he said, [3]
'Seven times a day I have praised you.' • And of the [4]
Night Office the same prophet said, 'At midnight I got
up to give you praise.'[2] • Let us therefore at these times [5]
give praise to our Creator 'for his righteous judgements',[3]
that is to say at Lauds, Prime, Terce, Sext, None,
Vespers and Compline, and at night let us get up to
praise him.

---

[1] Ps 118:164  [2] ibid:62  [3] ibid:164

# Chapter XVII How many Psalms are to be said at these Hours

1 • The order of the Psalmody at Matins and Lauds has already been dealt with; now we must consider the

2 remaining hours. • At Prime three Psalms should be

3 said, separately, and not under one *Glory be.* • The hymn is sung after the versicle, *O God come to my aid,*[1] before

4 beginning the Psalms. • When the three Psalms are finished there should be one lesson, a versicle, *Lord have*

5 *mercy* and the concluding prayers. • The Offices of Terce, Sext and None are to be carried out in the same way, thus: the opening verse, the hymn of the hour, the three Psalms, a reading and verse, *Lord have mercy* and the

6 concluding prayers. • If the community is large enough antiphons should be used; otherwise the Psalms are sung straight through.

7 • For the evening prayer meeting four Psalms with

8 antiphons will be enough. • After them a lesson should be recited, then a responsory, a hymn, a versicle, a canticle from the Gospels, the litany and the Lord's prayer at the end.

9 • For Compline the recitation of three Psalms, said

10 straight through without an antiphon, is enough. • After these there will be the hymn proper to this hour, a lesson, a versicle, *Lord have mercy*, and the blessing at the end.

Feb. 20
June 21
Oct. 21

---

[1] Ps 69:1

# Chapter XVIII In what order the Psalms should be said

Feb. 21
June 22
Oct. 22
• First should be said the verse, *O God come to my aid, Lord* 1
*make haste to help me,* and *Glory be;* then the hymn of the hour.

• Then at Prime on Sunday are to be said four stanzas 2
of Psalm 118; • at the remaining hours, namely Terce, 3
Sext and None, three stanzas of the same Psalm are to be said.

• At Prime on Monday three Psalms, namely 1, 2 and 4
6 are to be said, • and so on each day at Prime up to 5
Psalm 19, continuing till Sunday (exclusively); but note
that Psalms 9 and 17 are to be divided into two parts.
• In this way the Sunday Matins will always begin with 6
Psalm 20.

Feb. 22
June 23
Oct. 23
• At Terce, Sext and None on Mondays are to be said 7
the nine remaining stanzas of Psalm 118, three at each
hour. • Psalm 118 is thus finished on two days, Sunday 8
and Monday; • on Tuesday three Psalms are to be 9
chanted at each of Terce, Sext and None, from 119 to
127, nine Psalms in all. • And these Psalms are to be 10
repeated daily at the same hours until Sunday; but the
arrangement of hymns, readings and verses is to follow
the same pattern daily, • and on Sunday a new 11
beginning should be made with Psalm 118.

Feb. 23
June 24
Oct. 24
• Vespers are to be sung each day with four Psalms, 12
• beginning with Psalm 109 and ending with Psalm 147, 13
• but excluding those which are assigned to other hours, 14
namely Psalms 117–27, 133 and 142; • the rest are all to 15
be said at Vespers. • Since, however, there are three 16
Psalms too few, the longer Psalms of those just

mentioned, namely 138, 143, 144 are to be divided into
17  two. • On the other hand Psalm 116, being very short, is
to be joined with 115.

18  • This covers the order of the Psalms for Vespers: all
the other items, namely the reading, responsory, hymn,
versicle and canticle, are to be performed as we have laid
19  down above. • At Compline the same Psalms are to be
repeated daily, namely 4, 90 and 133.

20  • This settles the order of the Psalms during the day: Feb. 24
all the remaining Psalms are to be divided equally into (in L. Yr.)<br>June 25
the seven vigils of the night: twelve are to be allotted to Oct. 25
21  each night, • but dividing the Psalms of greater length.

22  • Nevertheless, we emphasise that if anyone is dis-
satisfied with this arrangement of the Psalms, he is to
23  organise them otherwise as he finds better; • he should,
however, see to it that the Psalter be recited every week,
24  starting anew from vigils of the Lord's Day. • For monks
who in the course of a week sing less than the Psalter
with its usual canticles manifest a service too slothful for
25  their dedicated state, • since we read that our holy
Fathers vigorously completed in a single day what it is to
be hoped we who are tepid may accomplish in a whole
week.

## Chapter XIX Recollection in chanting

Feb. 24
(or 25)
June 26
Oct. 26
• We believe that God is present everywhere, and that ¹
the eyes of the Lord are in every place, keeping watch on
the good and the bad;¹ • but most of all should we ²
believe this without any shadow of doubt, when we are
engaged in the work of God. • We should therefore ³
always be mindful of the prophet's words, 'Serve the
Lord with fear.'² • And again, 'Sing wisely.'³ • And yet ⁴,⁵
again, 'In the sight of the angels I will sing to you.'⁴ • We ⁶
must therefore consider how we should behave in the
sight of the Divine Majesty and his Angels, • and as we ⁷
sing our Psalms let us see to it that our mind is in
harmony with our voice.

---

¹ Pr 15:3  ² Ps 2:11  ³ Ps 46:8  ⁴ Ps 137:2

# Chapter XX Reverence at Prayer

1 • If we wish to bring anything to the attention of powerful men, it is only with humility and reverence that 2 we dare to do so. • How much more then should we present our supplications to the Lord God of all things with complete humility and devout purity of mind. 3 • Indeed we must grasp that it is not by using many words[1] that we shall get our prayers answered, but by 4 purity of heart and repentance with tears. • Prayer, therefore, should be short and pure, unless on occasion it be drawn out by the feeling of the inspiration of divine 5 grace. • In community, however, the prayer should be kept quite short, and when the superior gives the sign all should rise together.

Feb. 25 (or 26) June 27 Oct. 27

---

[1] Mt 6:7

# Chapter XXI Of the Deans of the Monastery

Feb. 26
(or 27)
June 28
Oct. 28
• If the community is rather large, brethren of good 1 reputation and holy way of life should be selected from among them and appointed deans. • They are to exercise 2 care over their deaneries in all respect according to the commandments of God and the instructions of their Abbot. • They should be chosen as deans who are such 3 that the Abbot may be able to share his burdens with them with confidence. • They should not be chosen 4 according to seniority but for their merits and their wisdom in teaching. • And if any of these deans, 5 becoming inflated with some form of pride, be found worthy of rebuke, he is to be corrected once, twice, indeed three times; but if he will not amend, he should be removed • and another who is worthy should be 6 substituted for him. • And we lay down the same 7 procedure for the Prior of the Monastery.

# Chapter XXIII Excommunication for Faults

Feb. 28
(or 29)
June 30
Oct. 30

• If any brother is found to be contumacious or 1
disobedient or arrogant or a grumbler or one who sets
himself up against some point of the Holy Rule or
despises the ordinances of his seniors, • he is to be 2
warned privately once or twice, according to our Lord's
command,[1] by his superiors. • If he does not amend his 3
ways, then he should be publicly rebuked before all. • If 4
he still does not improve let him undergo excommunication, if he understands the nature of this punishment.
• If, however, he is stubborn, he must undergo corporal 5
punishment.

---

[1] Mt 18:15-16

# Chapter XXIV How Excommunication is to be regulated

1 • Excommunication or disciplinary measures should be Mar. 1 July 1 Oct. 31
2 proportionate to the nature of the fault, • and the nature
3 of faults is for the Abbot to judge. • If then a brother is found to commit less serious faults he is to be deprived of
4 sharing in the common meal. • The rules for one who is thus excluded from the sharing in the common meal will be: he may not intone antiphon or Psalm in the oratory; nor may he read a lesson until he has made satisfaction.
5 • He must eat alone after the meal of the brethren.
6 • Thus if they eat at the sixth hour, he will eat in the
7 evening; • until having made adequate satisfaction he receives pardon.

# Chapter XXV Very serious Faults

• The brother who is guilty of a very serious fault is to be  1
suspended from sharing in the meals and also from the
oratory. • None of the brethren may associate with him  2
in companionship or conversation. • He is to be left alone  3
at the work assigned to him and to remain in penitent
grief as he reflects on the terrible sentence of the Apostle.
• 'This kind of man is handed over to bodily death, so  4
that his spirit may be saved for the day of the Lord.'[1]
• His food he should take alone in such measure and at  5
such time as the Abbot thinks most suitable for him;
• nor may he or the food that is given him receive a  6
blessing from anyone who passes by.

[1] I Co 5:5

48

# Chapter XXVI Unauthorised Association with the Excommunicated

1 • If any brother, acting without instructions from the Abbot, takes it upon himself to associate with an excommunicated brother in any way, or to talk with him, 2 or send him a message, • he must likewise undergo the punishment of excommunication.

Mar. 3
July 3
Nov. 2

# Chapter XXVII The Concern the Abbot must have for the Excommunicated

Mar. 4
July 4
Nov. 3

• The Abbot should carry out with the deepest concern his responsibility for the brethren who fall into sin, 'for it is not those who are in good health who need a doctor, but those who are sick.'[1] • For this reason he should, like a skilful doctor, use every possible remedy; for example he may send *senpectae* (that is, mature and wise brethren) • to give unofficial consolation to their wavering brother, and induce him to make humble satisfaction, and give him comfort, 'so that he is not overcome by too much sadness.'[2] • And so let it be as the Apostle also says, 'that love is reaffirmed towards him';[3] and everybody is to pray for him.

• It is indeed very important that the Abbot should show his concern, and make speed to employ his skill and energy, lest he lose one of the sheep entrusted to him. • For he must bear in mind that it is the care of sick souls that he has undertaken, not a despotic rule over healthy ones. • Moreover, he should fear the threats of the prophet, through whose words God says, 'What you saw to be fat you took, and what was weak you threw away.'[4] • And let him copy the loving example of the Good Shepherd who left the ninety-nine sheep on the mountains, and went away to search for the one that had gone astray; • and had such pity for its weakness that he deigned to lay it on his own sacred shoulders, and so carry it back to the flock.[5]

---

[1] Mt 9:12  [2] II Co 2:7  [3] ibid:8  [4] Ezk 34:3, 4  [5] Lk 15:4, 5

# Chapter XXVIII The Incorrigible

1 • If any brother who has been often corrected for some fault, and even been excommunicated, does not amend his way, he must receive harsher punishment, that is to
2 say, he must suffer a beating. • But if, even after this, he does not amend or if—which God forbid—he is so filled with pride as to want to defend his actions, then the
3 Abbot must act like a wise doctor. • If he has made use of poultices, of the ointments of his counsels, of the remedies of Divine Scripture, if he has come at last to the cautery of excommunication, and the blows of the rod,
4 • and if he now sees that his work is unavailing—let him make use of what is still greater: his own prayer
5 combined with that of all the brethren • that the Lord to whom nothing is impossible may work the salvation of the sick brother.

6 • But if even by this means he is not cured then the Abbot must employ the surgeon's knife, as the Apostle says, 'Drive out the wicked man from among you.'[1]
7 • And again, 'If the unfaithful one leaves you, let him
8 go,'[2] • for fear that one diseased sheep may infect the whole flock.

[1] Co 5:13  [2] I Co 7:15

# Chapter XXIX Whether Brethren who leave should be taken back

Mar. 6
July 6
Nov. 5

• If a brother has through his own wrong choice left the  1
monastery and wants to come back again, he must first
promise to make amendment for having left, • and then  2
let him be taken back in the lowest place as a test of his
humility. • If he goes away a second time, he may be  3
received back, and even a third time; but after that he
must realise that the path of return will not be granted
him again.

# Chapter XXX How Boys are to be corrected

1 • Disciplinary measures should be appropriate to every
2 age and intelligence: • hence when boys or youths or
others, incapable of understanding how serious a
3 punishment excommunication is, • commit offences,
such persons are to suffer additional fasts or painful
stripes, so that they may be cured.

Mar. 7
July 7
Nov. 6

# 2
# The Administration of the Monastery

# Chapter XXXI What Kind of Man the Cellarer of the Monastery should be

1 • As cellarer of the monastery should be chosen from the community one who is sound in judgement, mature in character, sober, not a great eater, not self-important, not turbulent, not harshly spoken, not an off-putter, not 2 wasteful, • but a God-fearing man who will be a father to 3 the whole community. • He is to have charge of all 4 affairs, • but he is not to act without the Abbot's 5, 6 approval, • and he must carry out his orders. • He must 7 not sadden the brethren. • If any brother happens to make an unreasonable demand of him, he should not upset him by showing contempt, but refuse the ill-8 advised petitioner with reasons modestly presented. • He must keep guard over his own soul, always bearing in mind that saying of the Apostle that he who has ministers well gains a good reputation for himself.[1] 9 • With all compassion he is to have care for the sick, the children, the guests and the poor, knowing for certain that in the day of judgement he will have to render 10 account for his treatment of them all. • He must regard the chattels of the monastery and its whole property as if 11 they were the sacred vessels of the altar. • He should 12 neglect nothing. • He must neither succumb to avarice nor be a wasteful squanderer of the monastery's goods; but he should conduct all his affairs with prudence and in accordance with the Abbot's instructions.

13 • It is essential that he should have humility and if he has nothing material to give, he should at least offer a 14 kind word of reply, • as it is written, 'A good word

[1] I Tm 3:13

57

surpasses the best gift.'[2] • He must keep under his own 15
care whatever the Abbot has entrusted to him, but he
should not undertake anything the Abbot has forbidden.
• He must provide the brethren with their regular 16
allowance of food, without fuss or keeping them waiting,
so as not to make for them an occasion of sin, keeping in
mind the divine saying about the retribution of him 'who
causes one of the little ones to sin.'[3] • If the community is 17
rather large, helpers should be given him, so that with
their aid he may himself tranquilly perform the office
entrusted to him.

• Whatever has to be asked for or given should be 18
asked for or given at suitable times, • so that no one may 19
be upset or saddened in the household of God.

---

[2] Sir 18:17   [3] Mt 18:6

# Chapter XXXII The Tools and Goods of the Monastery

1 • With regard to the monastery's material possessions such as tools, clothes, or other articles, the Abbot should put in charge of them brethren whose way of life and 2 character he can trust, • and then commit all these things to them, as he thinks best, for safe keeping, and 3 return after use. • The Abbot should keep a list of them so that when the brethren succeed one another in the tasks assigned to them he may know what is being 4 handed over or received back. • If anyone treats the property of the monastery in a dirty or careless manner, 5 he should be corrected • and if he does not amend, he should suffer punishment as laid down in the Rule.

Mar. 10
July 10
Nov. 9

# Chapter XXXIII Whether Monks may have personal Property

• It is of the greatest importance that this vice should be 1
totally eradicated from the monastery. • No one may 2
take it upon himself to give or receive anything without
the Abbot's permission • or to possess anything as his 3
own, anything whatever, books or writing tablets or pen
or anything at all; • for they are not allowed to retain at 4
their own disposition their own bodies or wills, • but they 5
must expect to receive all they need from the Father of
the monastery. And so it must not be allowed that
anyone should have anything which the Abbot has not
approved. • Everything should be common to all, as it is 6
written, and no one should call anything his own[1] or
treat it as such. • But if anyone is found to be 7
entertaining this wicked vice, he should be warned once,
and a second time; if he does not amend, he should
undergo punishment.

---

[1] Ac 4:32

# Chapter XXXIV Whether all should receive equal Shares

1 • It is written, 'Distribution was made to each as he had <sup>Mar. 12</sup>
2 need.'[1] • By this we do not say that favouritism should be <sup>July 12</sup> <sup>Nov. 11</sup>
shown to persons, far from it, but that infirmities should
3 be allowed for. • If someone needs less he should thank
4 God and not be upset; • if another needs more he should
be humble about his weakness, and not feel important on
5 account of the consideration shown him, • and thus all
6 members will be at peace. • Above all the bad habit of
grumbling must not make its appearance in any word or
7 gesture for any reason whatever. • If anyone is found
guilty of this, let him pay a heavy penalty.

---

[1] Ac 4:35

# Chapter XXXV The weekly Servers in the Kitchen

Mar. 13
July 13
Nov. 12
• The brethren should serve one another, and no one ¹ should be excused from kitchen duty except for sickness or because he is more usefully engaged elsewhere, • because through this service the reward of an increase ² in charity is gained. • For the weak, however, help ³ should be provided so that this duty may not cause them dejection. • Indeed all should have help according to the ⁴ size of the community and the location. • If the ⁵ community is rather large the cellarer should be excused from kitchen duty and, as we said before, also those who are engaged in more important tasks. • The test should ⁶ serve one another in turn with charity. • The one who is ⁷ finishing his week's duty does the washing on the Saturday; • he should also wash the towels with which ⁸ the brethren dry their hands and feet. • Moreover, he ⁹ who is ending his week's service together with him who is about to start should wash the feet of all.¹ • The outgoing ¹⁰ server must restore the crockery he has made use of, washed and intact to the cellarer, • and the cellarer must ¹¹ hand it over to the incomer, so that he knows what he is giving out and what he is getting back.

May 14
July 14
Nov. 13
• An hour before the meal, the weekly servers may ¹² each receive, in addition to the allotted quantity, a drink and some bread, • so that at the hour of the meal they ¹³ may serve their brethren without finding the work heavy or complaining. • On solemn days, however, they must ¹⁴ wait for the Mass. • On Sundays, immediately after ¹⁵ Lauds, the incoming and outgoing servers should prostrate themselves at the feet of all the brethren in the

¹ cf. Jn 13:15

16 oratory, and ask to be prayed for. • The outgoing server is to say the verse, 'Blessed are you Lord God for you
17 have helped and strengthened me.'[2] • When this has been said three times, and he has received a blessing, the incoming server follows and says, 'O God come to my
18 aid, Lord make haste to help me.'[3] • And this too is to be repeated three times by all. And so, having received the blessing, he begins his week's duty.

---

[2] Dn 3:28 combined with Ps 85:17    [3] Ps 69:1

# Chapter XXXVI Sick Brethren

Mar. 15
July 15
Nov. 14
• The care of the sick is to be given priority over everything else, so that they are indeed served as Christ would be served, • since he said of himself, 'I was sick and you visited me,'[1] • and 'What you did to one of the least, you did to me.'[2] • But the sick themselves must realise that it is to pay honour to God that they are being served, and they must not vex their brethren by asking for too much. • However, they must be borne with patience, because through them a very ample recompense is merited. • Therefore let the Abbot pay the greatest attention so that they suffer no neglect.

• For the sick brethren a separate room must be provided, and to serve them a brother who is God-fearing, diligent and zealous. • The use of baths should be allowed to the sick as often as is desirable, but to the healthy and the young this should not be granted very often. • Moreover, the eating of meat should be allowed to the sick who are in a weak condition, but when they are restored to health again, all should abstain from meat as usual. • The Abbot must take the greatest care that the sick are not neglected by the cellarer or those who serve them, for whatever is done wrong by his disciples concerns him.

[1] Mt 25:36   [2] ibid: 40

# Chapter XXXVII Old Men and Children

1 • Although human nature itself is drawn to feel sympathy Mar. 16
July 16
Nov. 15 for those in these stages of life, namely the old and children, yet it is right that the authority of the Rule also
2 should have regard to them. • Their weaknesses should at all times be taken into consideration, and the letter of the Rule should by no means be applied to them in
3 matters of food. • Indeed they should always be thought of compassionately, and they should have their meals before the prescribed times.

# Chapter XXXVIII The weekly Reader

Mar. 17
July 17
Nov. 16 • At the meals of the brethren there should always be 1 reading, but not by anyone who happens to take up the book. There shall be a reader for the whole week, and he is to begin on Sunday. • Let him begin after Mass and 2 Communion by asking the prayers of all that God may keep from him the spirit of vanity. • The reader himself 3 is to intone the verse, *O Lord open my lips, and my mouth shall proclaim your praise,*[1] and it is to be said three times by all. • And so, having received a blessing, let him begin to 4 read. • There is to be complete silence, so that no 5 whisper nor any voice other than that of the reader be heard there. • Whatever is wanted for eating and 6 drinking the brethren should pass to one another, so that no one need ask for anything. • If, however, something is 7 wanted, it should be asked for by some sign or sound rather than by speaking. • No one there present is to ask 8 any question about the reading or about anything, so that no opportunity for disturbance may arise; • unless 9 perhaps the superior wishes to say a few words for edification. • The weekly reader may take some refresh- 10 ment before he begins to read because of his Holy Communion and lest his fast should be a burden to him. • He is to take his meal afterwards with the weekly cooks 11 and servers.

• The brethren are not to read (or sing) in their order 12 of seniority but only those who edify the listeners.

---

[1] Ps 50:17

# Chapter XXXIX The Measure of Food

1 • We consider it to be enough for the daily meal, whether at the sixth or the ninth hour, that there should always be served two cooked dishes, to allow for the weaknesses 2 of different eaters; • so that if someone cannot eat of the 3 one dish he may still make a meal from the other. • So two cooked dishes should be enough for all the brethren. And if fruit or tender vegetables are to be had, a third 4 dish may be added. • A full pound of bread should be enough for a day, whether there is one meal or those of 5 dinner and supper. • If there is a supper a third of the pound of bread should be kept back by the cellarer and produced at that meal.

6 • If, however, their work is rather heavy, it will be in the Abbot's power and in his judgement to decide 7 whether it is expedient to increase the allowance. • But there must be no danger of over-eating, so that no monk 8 is overtaken by indigestion, • for there is nothing so opp- 9 osed to Christian life as over-eating, • as our Lord says, 'Take care that your hearts are not weighed down by 10 over-eating.'[1] • Young boys should not be given the same amount of food, but less than their elders. Frugality 11 should be the rule on all occasions. • All must refrain entirely from eating the flesh of quadrupeds, except for the sick who are really weak.

---

[1] Lk 21:34

# Chapter XL The Measure of Drink

Mar. 19
July 19
Nov. 18 • 'Each man has his special gift from God, one of one kind, another of another kind,'[1] • and hence it is with some diffidence that we fix the quantity of the food and drink of others. • But keeping in view the frailty of the weak, we think that half a pint of wine daily is enough for each. • Those, however, to whom God grants the capacity to abstain should know that they will have their own reward.

• If, however, local conditions or their work or the summer heat call for more, it must be for the superior to decide, but he must take care that neither excess nor drunkenness overtakes them. • For although we read that wine is not at all a drink for monks, yet, since in our days it is impossible to persuade monks of this, let us agree at least about this that we should not drink our fill, but more sparingly, • since 'wine leads even wise men into infidelity.'[2]

• When, however, local conditions bring it about that the above mentioned quantity is not available, but much less, or none at all, then those who live there should bless God and not grumble. • We lay special stress on this that the brethren remain free from grumbling.

---

[1] I Co 7:7  [2] Sir 19:2

# Chapter XLI At what Hours they should take their Meals

1 • From the holy feast of Easter until Pentecost the brethren are to have their dinner at midday, and their Mar. 20 July 20 Nov. 19
2 supper in the evening. • From Pentecost throughout the summer, unless the monks have work in the fields or the summer is oppressively hot, they should fast on Wednes-
3 days and Fridays until the ninth hour, • and on the other
4 days have dinner at midday; • but the midday meal may be kept up continuously throughout the week, if they have work in the fields or the summer heat is excessive; it
5 will be for the Abbot to decide. • For he is to modify and organise all their affairs in such wise that their souls may be saved, and that the brethren do whatever they do, without justification for grumbling.
6 • From 14 September, however, until the beginning of Lent they should always have their meal at the ninth hour.
7 • During Lent until Easter it should be in the evening.
8 • Vespers, however, should be sung at such an hour that the brethren will not need lamp-light for their meal,
9 but that everything will be finished by daylight. • Indeed at all seasons, the hour of supper or of the evening meal should be calculated so that everything may be done by daylight.

# Chapter XLII That no one may speak after Compline

Mar. 21
July 21
Nov. 20 • At all times monks ought to strive to keep silence but 1 particularly so during the hours of the night, • and this 2 means in all seasons, whether on days of fasting or on days of having a midday meal.

• If it is the latter season, then after rising from supper, 3 they should at once sit together and one of them should read the *Conferences* or the *Lives of the Fathers* or some other work which will edify the hearers, • but not the 4 Heptateuch or the Books of Kings; for this part of Scripture will not be helpful to those of weaker intelligence at this hour; they should, however, be read at some other time.

• If it has been a fast day, then after Vespers there will 5 be a short interval, and then they should assemble for the reading of the *Conferences* as we have said. • Four or five 6 pages should be read, or as many as the time permits; • and during this space of time for reading all come 7 together, including anyone who may have been occupied in a job assigned to him.

• So when all are assembled, they should say 8 Compline, and when they come out of Compline there should be no further permission for anyone to talk about anything. • If anyone is found transgressing this rule of 9 silence he is to be punished severely, • unless the need to 10 attend to guests has arisen, or it happens that the Abbot has given someone an order. • And in this case, too, the 11 matter is to be handled with all seriousness and genuine moderation.

# Chapter XLIII Latecomers to the Work of God or to Meals

1 • As soon as the signal for the Divine Office is heard, the
brethren must leave whatever they have been engaged in
2 doing, and hasten with all speed; • but with dignity, so
3 that foolishness finds no stimulus. • Nothing, therefore,
is to be given preference over the Work of God.

4 • If at the Night Office anyone arrives after the *Glory be* of Psalm 94, which for this reason we wish to be said altogether slowly and deliberately, he must not stand in
5 his place in the choir, • but last of all, or in a place set apart by the Abbot for such careless persons, so that they
6 may be seen by the Abbot and by everyone else, • until at the end of the Work of God he does penance by public
7 satisfaction. • We have thought it best that such persons should stand last or else apart, so that being shamed because they are noticed by everybody, they may for this
8 motive mend their ways. • For if they stay outside the oratory, there may be someone who will go back and go to sleep again, or maybe sit down outside the oratory and give himself up to gossip, and in this way an opportunity
9 is given to the evil one; • it is better that they go in and not lose the benefit of the whole Office: and they should mend their ways as well.

10 • At the Day Hours anyone who has not arrived at the Work of God after the versicle and the *Glory be* of the first Psalm that follows it, must take the last place as we have
11 laid down above, • nor may he take for granted permission to join the choir as they sing, until he has made satisfaction, unless the Abbot pardons him and
12 gives him permission; • nevertheless one guilty of this

71

fault should still make satisfaction.

• With regard to meals, the brother who does not 13 arrive before the verse, so that all may say the verse and pray together and go to their meal together, • that is the 14 brother who does not arrive either through carelessness or other fault, should be admonished twice for this behaviour. • If then he does not amend, he will not be 15 permitted to share the common meal, • but will be 16 separated from the companionship of the others to eat alone, and will be deprived of his portion of wine, until he makes satisfaction and improves. • The same applies 17 to anyone who absents himself from the verse said after the meal.

• Moreover, no one should be so bold as to take any 18 food or drink before or after the regular meal time. • But 19 if something is offered to a brother by the superior and he rejects it, then when he does want what he previously rejected, or something else, he is not to receive anything at all until he makes suitable satisfaction.

# Chapter XLIV How the Excommunicated are to make Satisfaction

1 • If, for serious faults, anyone is excommunicated from Mar. 24 July 24 Nov. 23 the oratory and from the common meals, he is to lie prostrate at the threshold of the oratory at the time when the Work of God is being carried out, saying nothing, 2 • but just lying there with his head to the ground at the 3 feet of them all as they come out of the oratory. • This he is to continue to do until the Abbot considers the 4 satisfaction to be enough. • When at the Abbot's bidding he comes in, he must cast himself at the feet of the Abbot and then at the feet of the others, that they may pray for him. 5 • Then following the Abbot's instructions he may be admitted into choir, in such position as the Abbot 6 decides, • but on condition that he does not presume to sing alone any Psalm or reading or anything else, until 7 the Abbot gives a fresh order. • Moreover, at every hour, when the Work of God is being finished, he is to cast himself on the ground in the place where he is standing. 8 • And so must continue to do penance, until the Abbot again orders him to stop making this satisfaction.

9 • With regard to those who for less serious faults are excommunicated from meals only, they are to make satisfaction in the oratory until the Abbot orders them to 10 stop. • They perform this penance until the Abbot gives his blessing and says, 'That is enough.'

# Chapter XLV Those who make Mistakes in the Oratory

Mar. 25
July 25
Nov. 24 • If anyone goes wrong in giving out a Psalm, responsory, 1
antiphon or reading, unless by making satisfaction he
humbles himself there before all, he must submit to
greater punishment; • for he refused to put right with 2
humility what he did wrong through lack of care. • And 3
boys should be beaten for such a fault.

74

# Chapter XLVI Those who commit Faults in other Matters

Mar. 26
July 26
Nov. 25

1 • If anyone while engaged in his work, in the kitchen, in the cellarer's offices, in the storeroom, in the bakery, in the garden or while engaged in any craft, or indeed 2 anywhere else, behaves badly • or breaks some article or 3 destroys it, or commits some excess, • he should come straightaway before the Abbot and the community, declare his transgression and make satisfaction. But if he 4 does not do this, • and the transgression becomes known through another, he must undergo a heavier penalty.

5 • However, if the failing be an interior sin, he should 6 declare it only to the Abbot or to spiritual fathers, • for they, knowing how to heal their own wounds, know how to heal those of others, without revealing them or making them known.

# Chapter XLVII The Signal for the Work of God

Mar. 27
July 27
Nov. 26
• To give the signal for the Work of God, whether by day 1
or by night, is the responsibility of the Abbot. He may do
it himself or he may lay the charge on a brother
sufficiently responsible to ensure that everything is
performed at the correct time. • The intoning of Psalms 2
and antiphons is to be done in turn after the Abbot by
those appointed. • No one should venture to sing or read 3
unless he can do it to the edification of his hearers • It is 4
to be done with humility, gravity and reverence, and by
appointment of the Abbot.

# Chapter XLVIII The daily manual Labour

1 • Idleness is the enemy of the soul. For this reason the Mar. 28<br>July 28<br>Nov. 27 brethren should be occupied at certain times in manual
2 labour, and at other times in sacred reading. • Hence we think that the times for these two duties may be arranged as follows:
3 • From Easter till 14 September, they should be set out in the morning and work at whatever is necessary from
4 the first hour till about the fourth. • From the fourth hour until about the sixth, they should be engaged in
5 reading. • After the sixth hour, and when they have had their meal, they may rest on their beds in complete silence, or if anyone has a mind to read, he may do so,
6 but in such a way as not to disturb anyone else. • None should be said rather early, at about the middle of the eighth hour, and then they should work again at
7 whatever their tasks are until Vespers. • If, however, local necessity or their own poverty compels them to work personally at gathering the harvest, they should not
8 be upset about this. • For then truly are they monks, if they live by the work of their hands, as did our Fathers
9 and the Apostles. • All their labours, however, should be kept under control on account of the less courageous.
10 • From 14 September until the beginning of Lent they Mar. 29<br>July 29<br>Nov. 28 should be free for reading till the end of the second hour.
11 • Then Terce should be said, and all should work at their
12 allotted tasks until None. • At the first signal for None every brother should detach himself from his work, so as
13 to be ready for the sounding of the second signal. • After their evening meal ·they should give themselves to reading or to studying the Psalms.

• In Lent, however, the hours for reading are from the 14
morning until the end of the third hour. Then until the
end of the tenth hour they should work at their allotted
tasks.
• And during these days of Lent everyone should receive 15
a book from the library, which he should read through
from the beginning. • These books are to be given out at 16
the beginning of Lent. • It is important that one or two 17
seniors should be appointed to go round the monastery
during the hours when the brethren are engaged in
reading, • to see whether perchance they come upon 18
some lazy brother who is engaged in doing nothing or in
chatter, and is not intent upon his book, and so not only
profitless to himself but leading others astray. • If such a 19
one is found (which we hope will not be the case) he
should be reprimanded once and a second time • and if 20
he does not amend, he should be punished in accordance
with the Rule, so that the others may be warned.
• Moreover, a brother should not be in the company of 21
another at the wrong time.

• On Sunday all should give themselves to reading, 22
except those to whom other duties have been assigned.
• But if anyone is so careless and idle that he is either 23
unwilling or unable to study or read, he must be given
some other task so as not to be unemployed.
• To the brethren who are in poor health or not 24
strong, the work or craft that is allotted should be such
as to keep them occupied, but not such as by its weight to
break them down or drive them away. Their lack of 25
strength is a matter for the Abbot's consideration.

# Chapter XLIX The Observance of Lent

1 • Although the monk's life ought at all seasons to bear a
2 Lenten character • such strength is found only in the few.
Therefore we urge the brethren to keep the days of Lent
3 with a special purity of life • and also at this holy season
4 to make reparation for the failings of other times. • This
reparation will be worthily performed if we guard
ourselves from all our faults and apply ourselves to
prayer with tears, to reading, to compunction of heart
5 and to abstinence. • Therefore at this season let us
increase in some way the normal standard of our
service, as for example, by special prayers, or by a
6 diminution in food and drink; • and so let each one
spontaneously in the joy of the Holy Spirit[1] make some
offering to God concerning the allowance granted him.
7 • Thus he may reduce food and drink for his body, or his
sleep, or his talkativeness or his looseness in speech, and
*so with the joy of spiritual desire, look forward to holy Easter.*

8 • But every brother should propose to the Abbot
whatever he intends to offer, and it should be performed
9 with his blessing and approval. • For anything done
without the permission of the spiritual father will be put
down to presumption and vainglory, and deserving no
10 reward. • Everything, therefore, must be carried out with
the approval of the Abbot.

---

[1] cf. Rm 14:17

# Chapter L Brethren who work far from the Oratory, or who are on a Journey

• Brethren whose work is at a considerable distance, and 1
who cannot reach the oratory at the right time— • and 2
the Abbot recognises this to be the case— • should 3
perform the Work of God in the place where they are
working, kneeling down in deep respect to God. • And 4
likewise those who are travelling should not allow the
hours prescribed for prayer to go unobserved, but they
should do their best to carry out their duties in God's
service and not neglect them.

# Chapter LI Brethren who go out on short Errands

1 • If a brother is sent out on some errand, and expects to return to the monastery the same day, he must not presume permission to eat outside the monastery, even if 2 the invitation is a very pressing one, • unless he has been 3 so instructed by the Abbot. • Anyone who does otherwise is to be excommunicated.

Apr. 2
Aug. 2
Dec. 2

81

# Chapter LII The Oratory of the Monastery

Apr. 3
Aug. 3
Dec. 3
• The oratory should correspond to its name, and not be 1 used for any other purpose, nor to store things. • When 2 the Work of God has been completed all are to go out noiselessly, and let reverence for God reign there. • So 3 that if a brother should have a mind to pray by himself, he will not be disturbed by the ill-conduct of anyone else. • Moreover, also on other occasions, if someone wishes to 4 make a private prayer, let him go in without hesitation and pray, not, however, aloud, but with tears, and the attention of his heart. • Anyone therefore, who is not 5 engaged on such a task, is not allowed to remain in the oratory after the Work of God, as we said above, lest someone else be disturbed.

# Chapter LIII The Reception of Guests

1 • All who arrive as guests are to be welcomed like Christ, for he is going to say, 'I was a stranger and you
2 welcomed me.'[1] • The respect due to their station is to be shown to all, particularly to those of one family with us in
3 the faith[2] and to pilgrims. • As soon as a guest is announced he should be met by the superior or by
4 brethren with every expression of charity, • and first of all they should pray together, and then greet one another
5 with the kiss of peace. • This kiss of peace should not be offered until after prayer has been said, since the devil
6 sometimes plays tricks. • When guests arrive or depart the greatest humility should be shown in addressing
7 them: • so, let Christ who is received in them be adored with bowed head or prostrate body.

8 • So when the guests have been welcomed they should be led to prayer, and then either the superior or
9 someone delegated by him should sit with them. • The Divine Law should be read to them for their edification, and after this every kindness should be shown to them.
10 • The superior may break the fast for the sake of a guest unless it happens to be an important fast day which
11 cannot be waived; • the brethren, however, should keep their accustomed fasts.

12 • The Abbot should give all the guests water to wash
13 their hands, • and with the whole community he should
14 wash their feet. • When they have done so, they should recite the verse, *We have received your mercy, O God, in the midst of your temple.*[3]

15 • Special care is to be shown in the reception of the

---

[1] Mt 25:35  [2] cf. Ga 6:10  [3] Ps 47:10

poor and of pilgrims, for in them especially is Christ received; for the awe felt for the wealthy imposes respect enough of itself.

Apr. 5
Aug. 5
Dec. 5
• The kitchen for the Abbot and guests should be 16 separate, so that when guests arrive at unforeseeable times (and they are always coming to a monastery) they may not disturb the brethren. • Two brethren capable of 17 performing this duty should take over this kitchen for a year. • Help should be given them as they need it, so that 18 they may serve without complaining, and also, when they have less work to do, they should leave their kitchen to work wherever they are bidden. • And this principle 19 applies not only to them but to all departments of the monastery: • help is to be provided for those in need, and 20 when they have spare time, they must obey their orders.

• Also, with regard to the guests' quarters, a brother 21 should be put in charge, whose soul is filled with the fear of God. • A sufficient number of beds should be kept 22 ready there. And let God's house be wisely cared for by wise men.

• No one without specific instructions is to associate or 23 converse with the guests. • If a brother should meet or 24 see one, he should, as we have said, give him a humble greeting, and then ask a blessing and go on his way, explaining that he is not allowed to converse with a guest.

84

# Chapter LIV Whether a Monk should receive Letters or other Gifts

1 • On no account may a monk, without the Abbot's Apr. 6 Aug. 6 Dec. 6 permission, either accept (or give) letters or offerings of blessed bread or small gifts of any kind whether from his
2 parents or other people or his brethren. • And if something is sent to him, even from his parents, he must not take upon himself to accept it before it has been
3 shown to the Abbot. • If the Abbot allows it to be accepted, it rests with him to decide to whom it shall be
4 given, • and the brother to whom it was sent must not be
5 upset, so that no opportunity is given the evil one. • If anyone should be headstrong enough to act otherwise he must submit to the discipline of the Rule.

# Chapter LV The Clothing and Footwear of the Brethren

Apr. 7
Aug. 7
Dec. 7

• Clothing should be given to the brethren according to the nature of the district where they live and the climate, • because in cold places more is needed and in warm ones less. • This is for the Abbot to consider. • It is our view that in temperate localities, it will be sufficient for monks if each has a cowl and a tunic— • the cowl should be woolly in winter, but thin or worn in summer— • and a scapular for work. For footwear he should have stockings and shoes. • The monks should not argue about the colour or coarseness of all these things, but accept what is available in the region where they live or can be bought cheaply.

• But the Abbot should take care about the size of these clothes, that they are not too short for those who use them, but of the right size. • Those who receive new clothes should always give the old ones back at once; they can be stored in the wardrobe for the benefit of the poor. • For it is sufficient for a monk to have two tunics and two cowls, to allow for wear at night and for washing: • more than that is superfluous, and should be taken away. • Their stockings also and anything that is old should be returned by them when they get new ones.

• Those who are sent on a journey should get drawers from the wardrobe, which they should wash and give back on their return. • And their cowls and tunics should be in rather better condition than those they usually have; they should get them from the wardrobe when they set out on this journey, and give them back on their return.

15 • For bedding, a mattress, a blanket, a coverlet and a
16 pillow are enough. • The beds should be frequently inspected by the Abbot as a precaution against private
17 possessions. • If anyone is found to have anything which was not given him by the Abbot, he is to undergo the
18 severest punishment; • and that this vice of personal ownership may be totally eliminated, everything necessary
19 should be given by the Abbot; • namely, a cowl, a tunic, stockings, shoes, a belt, a knife, a pen, a needle, a handkerchief and writing tablets, so that all excuses
20 about necessity are removed. • But the Abbot must always bear in mind the statement in the Acts of the Apostles that 'distribution was made to each according to his need.'[1]

21 • And so he must bear in mind the weakness of those
22 in need, but not the ill-will of the envious. • Indeed in all his decisions he must consider that God will repay.

---

[1] Ac 4:35

# Chapter LVI The Abbot's Table

Apr. 9
Aug. 9
Dec. 9 • The Abbot should always take his meals with the 1
guests and pilgrims. • Whenever there are no guests he 2
may at his own discretion invite to his table from among
the brethren those whom he wishes, • but one or two 3
seniors should always be left with the brethren for the
sake of discipline.

# Chapter LVII The Craftsmen of the Monastery

1 • If there are craftsmen in the monastery let them carry on their crafts in all humility, subject to the approval of
2 the Abbot. • But if any one of them becomes conceited because of his knowledge of his craft, which is 3 apparently bringing profit to the monastery, • he is to be taken away from his craft; nor is he to come back to it, unless, after he has shown humility, the Abbot gives him 4 a new permission. • If anything produced by the craftsmen is to be sold, those responsible for the transaction must take care not to venture to do anything 5 fraudulent. • They should always keep in mind the fate of Ananias and Sapphira, lest the death which those 6 persons incurred in the body, • they (and any who practise fraud in the affairs of the monastery) should themselves undergo in their souls.

7 • With regard to the prices charged, the sin of avarice 8 must not creep in; • but whatever is sold should be a 9 little cheaper than is possible for lay-persons, • 'so that God may be glorified in all things.'[1]

---

[1] I P 4:11

89

# 3
# The Renovation of the Monastery

# Chapter LVIII The Rules for receiving Brethren

1 • Easy admission is not to be granted to anyone as soon Apr. 11
2 as he applies to enter the monastic state, • but as the Aug. 11
Dec. 11
Apostle says, 'Test the spirits to see whether they are of
3 God.'[1] • But if the newcomer continues to knock on the
door, and it is seen that he puts up patiently with the
unkind replies and the difficulty of getting in, and that
after four or five days he is still persisting in his request,
4 • then let him be allowed to come in, and remain in the
5 guest quarters for a few days. • After that he should be in
the quarters of the novices, where they work and eat and
6 sleep. • And to them should be assigned a senior monk
who has the gift of winning souls, and he should pay
7 them the closest attention. • His care must be to find out
whether the newcomer sincerely seeks God, whether he is
earnest at the Work of God, in obedience and under
8 severe words. • All the things that are hard and
repugnant to nature in the way to God are to be
expounded to him.
9    • If he promises to persevere in his intention to
remain, after two months have passed, this Rule is to be
10 read to him from beginning to end, • and he is to be told,
'This is the law under which you are asking to live. If you
can keep it, come in; if, however, you cannot, freely
11 depart.' • If he still stands his ground, then he is to be led
to the above-mentioned novices' quarter, and once again
his patience under all kinds of trials is to be put to the
12 test. • After the passing of another six months, the Rule
is to be read to him so that he may know what he is
13 entering on. • If he still remains, after four months the

---
[1] I Jn 4:1

same Rule is to be read to him again. • Then, if, having 14
thought the matter over carefully, he promises to keep all
the rules, and to obey all the orders given him, he should
be admitted into the community. • He must, however, 15
realise that it is set down in the law of the Rule that from
that day onward he may not leave the monastery, • nor 16
cast off from his neck the yoke of the Rule which it was
open to him during all this lengthy deliberation to
decline or to undertake.

Apr. 12
Aug. 12
Dec. 12 • The one who is to be accepted into the community 17
must promise in the oratory, in the presence of all,
stability, conversion of life and obedience. • He is to do 18
this before God and all his saints, so that if he
subsequently behaves otherwise, he will know that he merits
condemnation by him the one whom he mocks. • With 19
regard to this promise he must write a petition, calling
on the names of the saints whose relics are there, and in
the name of the Abbot who is present. • This petition he 20
should write with his own hand or, if he is illiterate, it
must be written by another whom he has asked, and the
novice must make his sign on it. And he should place it
with his own hand on the altar. • When he has done so, 21
the novice himself straight away intones this verse, *Accept
me, Lord, according to your word, and I shall live, and you will
not disappoint me in my hope.*[2] • The whole community 22
repeats this verse three times, adding *Glory be to the Father*
at the end. • Then the brother novice prostrates himself 23
at the feet of each of the brethren, asking their prayers.
Then from that day onwards he is to be reckoned among
the community. • If he has any possessions, he must 24
either previously give them to the poor, or by means of a
formal donation give them to the monastery, keeping for

---

[2] Ps 118:116

25 himself nothing at all, • since he realises that from that
26 day he will have no power even over his own body. • At
once then in the oratory, let him be stripped of his own
clothes which he is wearing, and reclothed in those of the
27 monastery. • The clothes, however, which have been
taken from him must be placed in the wardrobe, and kept
28 there, • so that if at some later time he should agree to
the suggestion of the devil that he should leave the
monastery (which God forbid), he can be stripped of the
29 clothing of the monastery, before being sent away. • He
does not, however, get back the petition which the Abbot
took off the altar, but it is kept in the monastery.

# Chapter LIX The Sons of the Rich or the Poor who are offered

Apr. 13
Aug. 13
Dec. 13

• If it happens that a nobleman offers his son to God as a 1
monk, and the child is still of tender age, the parents
should make out the petition of which we have spoken.
• They should wrap this petition and the boy's hand 2
together with the Mass offering in the altar cloth and
offer him in that way. • As for their property, they must 3
in the same petition promise under oath that on no
occasion will they ever give him anything either
themselves or through an agent or by any other means,
nor will they afford him any opportunity for possessing
anything. • However, if they are unwilling to do this, and 4
want to have the merit of giving something as an alms to
the monastery, • they should make a donation to the 5
monastery of whatever they want to give; they may
reserve the income of it to themselves if they wish. • Thus 6
will be blocked every way by which expectation might
remain to deceive the child and (God forbid), lead him to
destruction, as we have learnt by experience.

• And poorer people may follow the same procedure. 7
• As for those who possess nothing at all, they may 8
simply make the petition and offer their son with the
Mass offering in the presence of witnesses.

# Chapter LX Priests who may want to live in the Monastery

1 • If anyone of the rank of priest asks to be taken into the Apr. 14<br>Aug. 14<br>Dec. 14 monastery, this should not be granted him too quickly.

2 • If, however, he is very persistent in his request, he must understand that he will have to observe the full discipline

3 of the Rule • and that no relaxation will be made for him, as the Scripture says, 'Friend, for what purpose have you

4 come?'[1] • Nevertheless it may be granted him to stand next to the Abbot, to pronounce blessings, and to celebrate Mass, provided the Abbot gives permission.

5 • Otherwise he must not take any privilege for granted, knowing that he is subject to the discipline of the Rule, and should give greater proofs of humility to all.

6 • Moreover, in the event of some appointment or other

7 monastic business coming up for consideration, • he must keep the position in the community which goes with the date of his entry into the monastery, and not the one granted him out of reverence for the priesthood.

8 • If any clerics should show the same desire to join the monastery, they should be placed in a slightly advanced position in the community, and they, too, must promise observance of the Rule and stability.

---

[1] Mt 26:50

# Chapter LXI How Travelling Monks are to be received

Apr. 15
Aug. 15
Dec. 15 • If a travelling monk should arrive from some far-off ₁ locality, and want to live as a guest in the monastery, • and be content with the customs that he finds there, ₂ and not disturb the community by making special demands, • but be quite content with what he finds, then ₃ let him be accepted for as long as he desires. • And if ₄ indeed with humble charity he reasonably criticises or points some things out, the Abbot should consider the matter carefully. For it may be that the Lord has sent him for this very purpose. • And if later on he wants to ₅ settle down permanently, this desire is not to be refused, especially as his way of life could be well known during his time as a guest.

Apr. 16
Aug. 16
Dec. 16 • If on the other hand during that time, he should be ₆ found demanding or a man of bad habits, not only should he not be allowed to join the community, • but he ₇ should be frankly told to go away, for fear that others should be corrupted by his unhappy condition.

• If, however, he is not the kind which deserves ₈ dismissal, not only should he be admitted to the community if he so petitions, • but he should be ₉ persuaded to stay so that others may be instructed by his example, • and because it is the one Lord we serve in ₁₀ every place, and the one King for whom the battle is fought. • Indeed if the Abbot sees him to be of sufficeint ₁₁ virtue, he may place him in a somewhat higher position. • In fact the Abbot may assign a more honourable ₁₂ position than that due to the day of entry not only to a monk, but to one coming from the above-mentioned ,

ranks of priests or clerics, if he recognises that their way
13 of life is worthy of such treatment. • The Abbot,
however, must take care never to accept permanently a
monk from another known monastery without either the
agreement of his Abbot or a letter of recommendation,
14 • since it is written, 'Do not to another what you would
not want done to yourself.'[1]

---

[1] Tb 4:16

# Chapter LXII The Priests of the Monastery

Apr. 17
Aug. 17
Dec. 17
• If an Abbot wishes to have a priest or deacon ordained 1
for his service, he should choose from his monks one who
is fit to exercise the priesthood. • He who is ordained, 2
however, must beware of elation or pride • and he should 3
not take upon himself any work that has not been
committed to him by the Abbot.

He should realise that he is all the more bound to
submit to monastic discipline. • Nor on account of his 4
priesthood should he forget the obedience and the
discipline of the Rule, but he should go forward more
and more towards God.

• Let him always keep the position corresponding to 5
his entry into the monastery, • except when officiating at 6
the altar, unless the choice of the community and the will
of the Abbot promote him to a higher station on account
of the merit of his life. • He should realise that he is 7
bound by the rule laid down for deans and priors; • if he 8
presumes to behave otherwise, the judgement will be
passed not *on the priest but on the rebellion.* • If after 9
frequent warnings he does not mend his ways, the Bishop
also should be called in as a witness against him. • If, 10
even so, he does not amend and his faults are manifest,
he must be expelled from the monastery — • that is if his 11
stubbornness is such that he will neither submit nor obey
the Rule.

# Chapter LXIII The Order of the Community

1 • The time of their entering monastic life, their personal Apr. 18
merits, and the decision of the Abbot, shall decide the Aug. 18
Dec. 18
2 order which they keep in the monastery. • Yet the Abbot
must not upset the flock entrusted to him, nor should he
make any unjust arrangement as though he were free to
3 give orders as he pleases, • for he must always bear in
mind that he is going to have to render an account of all
4 his decisions and actions. • In the order, then, which he
has laid down, or which they otherwise have among
themselves, shall the brethren come to the kiss of peace,
or to Communion, or intone a Psalm or occupy their
5 place in choir. • In no circumstances or places is age to
6 decide order or have any bearing upon it, • for the
youthful Samuel and Daniel acted as judges over their
7 elders. • Therefore, with the exception of those whom, as
we have said, the Abbot has promoted or degraded for
definite reasons, the rest are to take their places
according to the time of their coming to the monastery;
8 • for example, one who has entered the monastery at the
second hour is to know that he is junior to him who
9 entered at the first, whatever his age or dignity. • For the
boys, however, all have the task of keeping order
wherever they are.

10 • Juniors, therefore, must show respect for their Apr. 19
11 seniors, and seniors must love their juniors. • In calling Aug. 19
Dec. 19
one another by name it is not allowed to anyone to use
12 the name alone • seniors should address their juniors by
the name of brother; juniors should address their seniors
as *Nonnus*, by which is signified the reverence due to a
13 father. • The Abbot, however, as he is believed to act in

101

the place of Christ, should be called Lord and Abbot, not because he demands these titles, but for the honour and love of Christ. • He himself must bear this in mind, 14 and show himself worthy of such honour.

• Whenever the brethren meet one another, the junior 15 should seek a blessing of the elder. • A younger monk 16 should rise and offer the seat to an older one if he passes by, nor should he venture to sit down again, unless the older one tells him to, • so that it may be as it is written, 17 'Forestall one another in paying honour.'[1]

• Children and youths are to keep their places, in good 18 order, in the oratory and at table. • Out of doors also and 19 anywhere at all they should be under supervision and discipline, until they reach an age that can understand.

---

[1] Rm 12:10

# Chapter LXIV The Institution of the Abbot

1 • This principle must always be kept in mind in the Apr. 20<br>Aug. 20<br>Dec. 20 institution of the Abbot: he should be appointed whom the united community chooses in the fear of God, or whom a smaller part of the community chooses with the 2 sounder judgement. • He who is to be appointed must be chosen on account of his virtuous life and wise teaching, 3 even if he is the last in order in the community. • So that even if (may it not happen!) the whole community should with one accord elect a person who will connive at 4 their defects, • and if these defects somehow become known to the Bishop to whose diocese the place belongs, 5 and to the local abbots or christians, • they should put a stop to this plot of wicked men, and set a worthy steward 6 over the household of God. • And they should know that they will receive a good reward if they act with a pure intention and zeal for God, and that on the other hand it would be sinful to neglect their duty.

7 • When he has been instituted, the Abbot should Apr. 21<br>Aug. 21<br>Dec. 21 always bear in mind what a burden he has undertaken, and to whom he will have to render an account of his 8 stewardship. • He should know, too, that he ought to be of profit to his brethren rather than just preside over 9 them. • He ought, therefore, to be learned in the divine law, so that he may know it well, and that it may be for him a store whence he draws forth new things and old. He should be a chaste man, temperate and merciful. 10 • He should always prefer mercy to judgement,[1] that he 11 may also obtain mercy. • Let him hate sin, let him love the brethren.

---

[1] Jm 2:13

103

• In correcting he should act prudently, and not 12
overdo it; for fear that as he tries too hard to get rid of the
rust, the pot gets broken. • Also he should always 13
mistrust his own frailty, and remember that the bruised
reed is not to be broken. • In saying these things, we do 14
not imply that he should allow vices to flourish, but that
he should eliminate them prudently and with charity, as
seems best in each case, as we have already said. • And it 15
should be his aim to be loved rather than feared. • Let 16
him not be restless or anxious, not over-demanding and
obstinate, not a perfectionist or full of suspicion, or he
will never have any peace. • In giving his instructions he 17
should have forethought and consideration; and whether
the instructions which he gives concern God's affairs or
temporal ones, let him be discerning and moderate,
• bearing in mind the discretion of holy Jacob who said, 18
'If I cause my flocks to be overdriven, they will all die in
one day.'[2]

• Taking to heart therefore these and other examples 19
of discretion, the mother of virtues, he should so regulate
everything that the strong may desire to carry more, and
the weak are not afraid.

• And, especially, he must in every respect keep this 20
present Rule • so that having fulfilled his ministry well, 21
he may hear from the Lord the same words as that good
servant who gave his fellow servants wheat in due
season, • 'Truly I say to you, he will place him over 22
everything he owns.'[3]

---

[2] Gn 33:13   [3] Mt 24:47

# Chapter LXV The Prior of the Monastery

1 • It happens fairly often that serious scandals occur in
2 monasteries because of the appointment of a Prior; • for
there are those who, swelling up with an evil spirit of
pride, consider themselves second abbots, act like tyrants
and nourish scandals and quarrels in the community.
3 • This happens especially in places where the Prior is
appointed by the same Bishop or by the same abbots as
4 appoint the Abbot of the monastery. • It is easy to see
how unwise this is: for from the very beginning of his
appointment the Prior is given grounds for waxing
5 proud, • since his thoughts suggest to him that he is
6 exempt from the Abbot's authority, because, • 'You have
been appointed by the same persons as the Abbot.'
7 • Hence arise envy, quarrels, detraction, rivalries, dis-
8 sensions and disorders; • for while the Abbot and Prior
are in opposition to each other, of necessity their own
9 souls are endangered by this quarrelling, • and also those
under their authority, seeking favour from one side or the
10 other, head for perdition. • The evils arising from such a
dangerous state of affairs are due primarily to those who
have been the originators of such a disorder.

11 • For this reason we think it expedient for the
preservation of peace and charity that the making of
appointments in the monastery should depend on the
12 Abbot's judgement • and, if it is possible, that all the
business of the monastery should be carried on through
deans, under the control of the Abbot, as we have
13 already laid down. • Thus no one may wax proud over
what is committed to many.
14 • If, however, local conditions require it, or the

Apr. 22
Aug. 22
Sept. 22

Apr. 23
Aug. 23
Dec. 23

community makes a reasonable and humble request, and the Abbot judges it to be expedient, • then the Abbot 15 himself should appoint as his Prior whomsoever he chooses after taking the advice of God-fearing brethren. • For his part the Prior is to perform respectfully 16 whatever functions the Abbot lays upon him, and do nothing contrary to his will or arrangements. • For 17 inasmuch as he has been placed over others, he should the more carefully keep the precepts of the Rule. • If it 18 should turn out that the Prior has serious faults or, deceived by vanity, acts arrogantly, or it turns out that he is a belittler of the Holy Rule, he should be verbally rebuked up to four times; • if he does not then change his 19 ways, he should be punished according to the disciplinary code. • If, however, he does not amend even so, 20 then he must be deposed from his office as Prior, and another who is suitable for it be put in his place. • And if 21 afterwards he does not live quietly and obediently among the community, he should even be expelled from the monastery.

• The Abbot should, however, bear in mind the 22 account he must render to God for all his decisions, for fear that the flame of jealousy or evil zeal burn in his soul.

# Chapter LXVI The Doorkeepers of the Monastery

1 • At the gate of the monastery, a wise old man is to be
posted, one capable of receiving a message and giving a reply, and whose maturity guarantees that he will not
2 wander round. • This doorkeeper should have a cell near the gate, so that persons who arrive may always find
3 someone at hand to give them a reply. • As soon as anyone knocks, or a poor man calls out, he should
4 answer 'Thanks be to God' or 'God bless you'. • Then with all the gentleness that comes from the fear of God, he should speedily and with the warmth of charity attend to the enquirer.

5 • If the doorkeeper needs it, he should have a younger brother to help him.

6 • If it is possible, the monastery should be organised so that all its needs, that is to say things such as water, a mill, a garden, and various crafts, may be met within its
7 premises, • so that the monks have no need to wander round outside it, for that does not profit their souls at all.

8 • This Rule we wish to be read frequently in the community, so that none of the brethren may plead ignorance of it.

# Appendix

# Chapter LXVII Brethren sent on a Journey

1 • Brethren who are being sent on a journey are to Apr. 25
Aug. 25
Dec. 25 commend themselves to the prayers of all the brethren
2 and of the Abbot; • and in the final prayer of the Work of God there should be a commemoration of all who are
3 absent. • When brethren return from a journey, at all the canonical hours of the day on which they return, they should lie prostrate on the floor of the oratory, as the
4 Work of God comes to an end, • and ask for the prayers of all,[1] for any faults that may have overtaken them on their journey, such as the sight or hearing of an evil thing
5 or idle chatter. • No one should venture to tell another anything he may have seen or heard while outside the
6 monastery, for that does much harm. • But if anyone does this he must undergo punishment according to the
7 Rule. • The same thing applies to anyone who dares to go out of the enclosure of the monastery, or to go anywhere, or do anything, although of small importance, without the approval of the Abbot.

---

[1] cf Tb 11:7 (Vulg.)

# Chapter LXVIII If a Brother is set impossible Tasks

Apr. 26
Aug. 26
Dec. 26 • If it should happen that burdensome or impossible 1
tasks are imposed on one of the brethren he should
indeed accept with complete calm and obedience the
command of the one who so orders, • but if he sees that 2
the weight of the burden quite exceeds the limits of his
strength, he should quietly and at a suitable moment
explain to his superior the reasons why he cannot do it,
• not in a proud way nor with the spirit of resistance, or 3
contradiction. • But if after his explanations the one in 4
authority remains firm in requiring what he has ordered,
the junior must understand that this is what is best for
him, • and let him lovingly trust in God's aid, and so 5
obey.

# Chapter LXIX That in the Monastery one must not defend another

1 • Let it be noted that in the monastery no monk may assume the right to defend or act as a kind of protector to
Apr. 27
Aug. 27
Dec. 27
2 another for any reason whatever, • even if they are
3 connected by a bond blood-relationship. • Monks must not presume to do this in any way, for from it may arise the
4 possibility of very grave scandals. • If anyone offends in this respect he must be sharply dealt with.

# Chapter LXX That no one may hit another

Apr. 28
Aug. 28
Dec. 28
• All outbreaks of self-assertiveness are to be avoided in ₁
the monastery. • We therefore lay down that no one is ₂
allowed to excommunicate or strike any of his brethren,
unless the Abbot has given him authority to do so.
• 'Those who offend must be rebuked in the presence of ₃
all, so that the rest may be warned.'[1] • Care, however, ₄
and supervision are to be shown by everyone with regard
to the discipline of children up to fifteen years of age,
• yet with all moderation and good sense. • With regard ₅ ₆
to those who are older than that, if anyone presumes to
take action without the Abbot's instruction, or gets angry
and behaves without discretion to the children also, he
must submit to the discipline of the Rule, • for it is ₇
written, 'Do not to another what you would not have
done to yourself.'[2]

---

[1] Tm 5:20  [2] Tb 4:16

114

# Chapter LXXI That the Brethren obey one another

1 • The goodness of obedience is not to be shown only Apr. 29 Aug. 29 Dec. 29 through obedience to the Abbot, but the brethren should
2 also obey each other, • in the knowledge that by this path
3 of obedience they will draw nearer God. • The commands of the Abbot or of the superiors appointed by him must come first and we do not allow personal demands to be
4 attended to before them, • but otherwise all the younger monks should obey the older ones with all love and care.
5 • And if anyone is found to be contentious, he should be
6 corrected. • And if, for any reason at all, a brother is
7 corrected in any way by the Abbot or by an elder, • or if he perceives that the feelings of any elder have been
8 roused to anger against him, even slightly, • he should at once and without delay prostrate himself at his feet and lie there in sign of reparation until the rift is healed by a
9 blessing. • If anyone is too proud to do this, he must either undergo corporal punishment or, if he is contumacious, he must be put out of the monastery.

# Chapter LXXII On the good Zeal which Monks ought to have

Apr. 30
Aug. 30
Dec. 30

• As there is an evil zeal rooted in bitterness which ¹ separates from God and leads to hell, • so there is a good ² zeal which separates from vice and leads to God and to eternal life. • This, therefore, is the zeal which monks ³ should practise with the most ardent love, • in other ⁴ words, they should forestall one another in paying honour.[1] • They should with the greatest patience make ⁵ allowance for one another's weaknesses, whether physical or moral. • They should rival one another in practising ⁶ obedience. • No one should pursue what he thinks ⁷ advantageous for himself, but rather what seems best for another. • They should labour with chaste love at the ⁸ charity of the brotherhood. • They should fear God. ⁹ • They should love their Abbot with sincere and humble ¹⁰ charity. • They should prefer nothing whatever to ¹¹ Christ.

    • May he bring us all alike to life everlasting. ¹²

---

[1] Rm 12:10

116

# Epilogue

# Chapter LXXIII That the whole Keeping of Justice[1] is not covered by this Rule

May 1
Aug. 31
Dec. 31

• We have written this Rule so that by following it in 1 monasteries, we may to some extent show that we lead blameless lives and possess a beginning of the monastic way of life. • In addition there are for him who would 2 hasten to the perfection of the monastic ways the doctrines of the holy Fathers, which, if a man keeps them, will lead to the height of perfection. • For is not 3 every page of the Old or New Testament, every word of the Divine Author, a most direct rule for our human life? • Does not every book of the Catholic Fathers proclaim 4 that we should make our way by the most direct path to our Creator? • There are also the *Conferences,* and 5 *Institutes,* and the *Lives of the Fathers,* and the *Rule* of the holy Father Basil. • What are these works but aids to the 6 attainment of virtue for good-living and obedient monks? • But to us who are slothful, who live badly and who are 7 negligent, they bring a blush of shame. • Whoever you 8 are, then, who are hurrying forward to your heavenly fatherland, do you with Christ's help fulfil this little Rule written for beginners; • and then you will come at the 9 end, under God's protection, to those heights of learning and virtue which we have mentioned above. Amen.

[1] Cf. Mt 3:15

118